Introduction to the iPad :
A Guided Tour

iOS/iPadOS 16 Edition

© 2023 iTandCoffee

This Guide reflects screens, options and functionality found in iOS 16 & iPadOS 16.

Special Sales and Supply Queries

For any information about buying this title in bulk quantities, or for supply of this title for educational or fund-raising purposes, contact iTandCoffee email **enquiry@itandcoffee.com.au** or call **1300 885 420.**

iTandCoffee classes and private appointments

For queries about classes and private appointments with iTandCoffee, call **1300 885 420** or email **enquiry@itandcoffee.com.au.**

Introduction to the iPad and iPhone
A Guided Tour

TABLE OF CONTENTS

Introduction to the iPad and iPhone
A Guided Tour

TABLE OF CONTENTS

Introduction to the iPad and iPhone
A Guided Tour

TABLE OF CONTENTS

Introduction to the iPad and iPhone
A Guided Tour

TABLE OF CONTENTS

Introduction to the iPad and iPhone
A Guided Tour

TABLE OF CONTENTS

Introduction to the iPad and iPhone
A Guided Tour

TABLE OF CONTENTS

Introduction to the iPad and iPhone
A Guided Tour

TABLE OF CONTENTS

Before we start ...

In this book, we will be talking about <u>both</u> the iPad and the iPhone, covering devices that do have a Home Button (the round button on the front of your device) and those that don't.

Don't worry whether you have an iPad or iPhone – nearly all functions are available on both devices. The main difference is in size and (sometimes) position of options, and that your phone can make phone calls. Although, in saying that, your iPad can also make calls using apps like Facetime, WhatsApp, or Messenger!

Generally, we will be looking at the symbols and functions that apply to the latest version of the 'operating system' that runs your i-Device. This is called iOS 16 for iPhones, and iPadOS 16 for iPads - released in September and October 2022 respectively. The previous version of the operating system was called iOS/iPadOS 15.

Some people are still using an earlier version of the operating system on their older Apple mobile device, where they may be unable to upgrade their devices any further due to the age of their device. We will not be covering these earlier versions as part of this guide, as they are covered in previous editions. Contact <u>sales@itandcofee.com.au</u> if you are interested in purchasing one of our previous editions of this guide.

If you see a '1' sitting on top of your **Settings** app icon, this often means you can update or upgrade your device to the latest version of your devices operating system, iOS. (In saying this, the '1' may be alerting you to something else that needs attention.)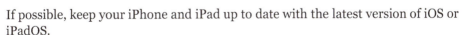

If possible, keep your iPhone and iPad up to date with the latest version of iOS or iPadOS.

We have more information about iOS/iPadOS versions and updates/upgrades towards the end of this book.

Let's first take a quick look at the layout of an iPhone and iPad including the main switches you will find on them.

New in iOS/iPadOS 16 ...

In this book, we have not attempted to cover *all* of the changes that arrived in iOS/iPadOS 16, as many relate to apps that we cover in separate books. And there are so many changes!

There are still lots of useful changes that *are* referred to in this guide – and below provides a useful index for those wishing to check out what's changed.

For anyone looking to explore all the changes delivered in iOS and iPadOS 16, here is Apple's list:

- iPhone (iOS 16): www.apple.com/au/ios/ios-16/features/

- iPad (iPadOS 16): www.apple.com/au/ipados/ipados-16/features/

Let's take a look at the iPhone

iPhone _with_ Home Button

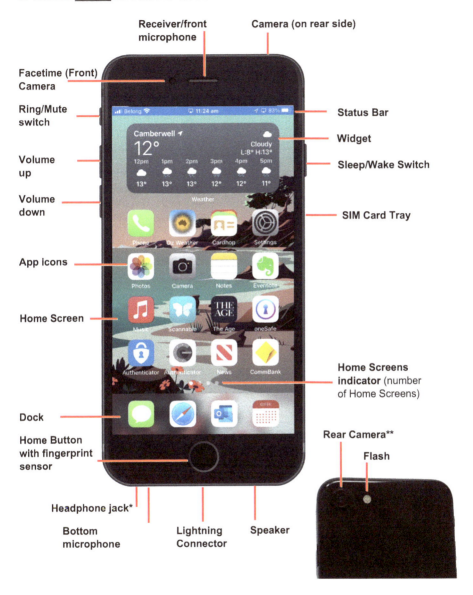

Receiver/front microphone

Camera (on rear side)

Facetime (Front) Camera

Ring/Mute switch

Status Bar

Widget

Volume up

Sleep/Wake Switch

Volume down

SIM Card Tray

App icons

Home Screen

Home Screens indicator (number of Home Screens)

Dock

Home Button with fingerprint sensor

Rear Camera**

Flash

Headphone jack*

Bottom microphone

Lightning Connector

Speaker

*iPhone 7, 8 and newer iPhone SE do not have a headphone jack

**iPhone 7 Plus, 8 Plus have 2 cameras on the back

Let's take a look at the iPhone

iPhone <u>without</u> Home Button

Receiver/front microphone

Camera (on rear side)

Facetime (front) Camera

Status Bar

Ring/Mute switch

Volume up

Volume down

App icons

Home Screen

SIM Card Tray

Dock
(for your most-used apps

Widget (cut down version of an app showing snippet of information)

Sleep/Wake Switch*

Home Screens indicator (number of Home Screens) OR Spotlight Search (new in iOS 16)

Rear Camera**

Flash

Bottom microphone   Lightning Connector   Speaker

* iPhone SE (first generation) has the Sleep/Wake Switch at top right instead of on the side – as shown for iPad below.

**The Rear Camera configuration shown here is from an iPhone 12 Pro. Different configurations apply for other models.

Let's take a look at the iPad

iPad <u>with</u> Home Button

Speakers

Front-facing camera

Speakers

Sleep/Wake Button

Up } Volume
Down { Controls

Dots showing number of home screens

The Dock (for your most-used apps)

Home Button

Speakers

Speakers

Lightning Connector

The rear camera may look different on your iPad – but here is where it is positioned

Let's take a look at the iPad

iPad <u>without</u> Home Button

Front-facing camera

Speakers

Speakers

Wake/Sleep Button
PLUS
Fingerprint Sensor (iPad Air)

Up { Volume
Down { Controls

Magnetic
dock for
Apple Pencil

Dots
showing
number of
home
screens

The Dock
(for your
most-used
apps)

Speakers

USB-C
Connector

Speakers

Flash

The rear camera configuration differs for the iPad Pro and
iPad Air, but the position is as shown in this image on
right.

The iPad Pro has a flash included with the rear camera
– the iPad Air does not.

Some Terminology

The world of technology brings such a huge amount of tech jargon, a language that can seem so foreign. Here are just some of the terms that we will be referring to in this guide, providing a quick reference to descriptions of these terms.

Term	Description
Apps	Short for 'Application' – a 'software program' that performs a particular function or set of functions
	Your device comes with a set of standard apps – you can add more.
	Some examples of standard apps are **Mail** (for emailing), **Safari** (for web browsing), **Camera** (for taking photos), **Photos** (for viewing photos), **Notes** (for jotting **notes** and lists), **Contacts** (your address book) and **Calendar** (your diary).
Home Screen	The **Home Screen** is the screen showing your apps
	If you have more apps than will fit on a single screen, you will have multiple home screens, accessed by swiping right to left and vice-versa.
Home Button	The **Home Button** is the one and only button on the front of some models of iPad & iPhone.
	Older devices have a rounded square on this Home Button.
	Newer devices with a Home Button don't have this square. Instead, they have a **Touch Sensor** (as shown), to unlock the device with your fingerprint (Touch ID).
	For those devices that don't have a Home Button, the 'Swipe Up' gesture is the equivalent of pressing once on the Home Button – and Face ID (facial recognition) replaces Touch ID for unlocking your device.

Some Terminology

Term	Description
Lock Screen	The screen that appears when you 'wake up', or first turn on your device, is the **Lock Screen**. Its purpose is to prevent inadvertent activations of apps and features (eg. 'pocket dialling'). It shows the current time and may also show some recent notifications. You can customise your Lock Screen by putting one of your own photos on that screen. With iOS 16, the Lock Screen can also be set up to show some things called 'widgets' – and you can have more than one Lock Screen on your iPhone.
Operating System	An operating system (OS) manages the operation of a computer or mobile device, looking after the apps and 'hardware' of the device and how they operate together. It provides standard services that apps can use (and more). Operating Systems that you may have heard of for other types of computers and mobile devices are Windows, Android, macOS, Linux. Each operating system is different and specifically developed to work on a particular type of device.
iOS	**iOS** is the Operating System that controls iPhones and older iPads. The number associated with iOS is the version number.
iPadOS	**iPadOS** is the Operating System that controls iPads and was first introduced as iPadOS 14 in 2020. (Note. Older iPad that cannot run iPadOS 14 still use iOS.)
Updates and Upgrades	Apple regularly updates and upgrades iOS. **Upgrades** are usually yearly (e.g. iOS 15 to iOS 16) and bring significant changes and new features **Updates** are intermittent throughout the year (e.g. iOS 16.0.1 was a 'fix' release, 16.2 brought more significant changes)

Some Terminology

Term	Description
Widgets	Widgets are larger icons from apps that show information from that app. 
	As an example, the Weather widget (right) can show on your Home Screen and include latest weather information.
	With iOS 16, some widgets can also appear on the iPhone's Lock screen.
Wi-Fi	One of the ways your iPad or iPhone can access the internet is using a Wi-Fi network.
	To have a Wi-Fi network, you need either a **fixed internet connection to your home** (or premises), or a 'mobile' Wi-Fi device that can connect to the 'Mobile Data' network (see next section). In more remote areas, internet can be provided via Satellite dishes on the roof.
	In Australia, internet services are most typically provided by the National Broadband Network (NBN).
	(We discuss the different types of fixed internet connection in more detail in our **Getting Connected** guide.)
	A **Modem** is required to access the internet that is connected to your premises and provide the internet connection to other devices. 
	Connecting a device called a **Router** to the modem sends a Wi-Fi signal to a range of 20-50m, allowing devices like iPads, iPhone, laptops, printers, TVs, etc. to connect to the router, and to its internet connection.
	Sometimes, the **router and modem are combined** into a single modem/router device (although the arrival of NBN has meant that many of us have two devices again - an NBN modem, attached to a router that our Telco provides us).
	A router provides one or more **Wi-Fi Networks** and each **Wi-Fi Network** has a network name. (Most routers will provide a 2.4ghz and 5ghz network. The 2.4ghz network offers

Some Terminology

Term	Description

broader range, but slower speed. The 5ghz network offers faster speed, but has less range.)

Your device must 'join' the Wi-Fi network to use the internet it provides. This is done from the **Settings** app on your device. Most Wi-Fi networks need a **Password** to gain access - the owner of the network must give you that password.

Your home's Router will have a 'default' network name (also known as an SSID) and password (or Network Key).

You may have business card sized card or magnet that shows these details. They are also usually shown on bottom of the router itself.

Mobile Data, Cellular Data, 3G, 4G
Another option for internet access is using **a Mobile Data Network** (also called a **Cellular Data Network, 3G, 4G or 5G Network**)

Such networks provide Wireless internet, supplied by mobile phone towers to a wide area – so that you can access the internet when you are not at home.

A device must have a **SIM Card** that has been activated with a mobile service provider. Newer devices can also have technology called an **eSIM**.

An eSIM is an embedded SIM built into the device - rather than (or in addition to) a separate physical SIM.

On the iPhone XR, XS, 11, 12, 13, and 14, the eSIM built into these devices allows you to have two separate mobile numbers/plans associated with your iPhone – great for separating personal/business calls, or for having an overseas number when you travel. (Note. Other iPhone models don't include an eSIM – only a physical SIM Card capability.) In the US, Apple has also introduced an 'eSIM only' iPhone, one that does not include any physical SIM.

Some Terminology

Term	Description

Another option for supplying internet to any devices is to use a separate Mobile Broadband Modem, to provide access to the internet via the Mobile Data Network – an example of which is shown below (although such modems can be in a huge variety of shapes and sizes).

Another alternative is to 'borrow' the internet from your iPhone or iPad with SIM card (or other internet-connected smartphone/tablet), using something called your 'personal hotspot' or 'tethering'. We touch on this later in this guide.

Charging your iPad and iPhone

Most iPads and iPhones come with a power adaptor and USB 'Lightning' cable. For the new iPads, the Lightning cable has been superseded by the USB-C cable (see examples of both on right).

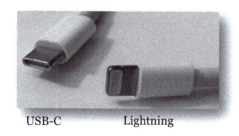

The iPad and iPhone power adaptors (that you plug into a power socket) look different, with the iPhone adaptor a smaller size compared with the iPad adaptor (see examples below).

USB-C   Lightning

iPad adaptor   iPhone Adaptor & USB Cable

The USB '**Lightning**' cable (or USB-C cable) that comes with the adaptor can be disconnected from the wall adaptor and used to plug the iPad or iPhone into a computer (or into a different power adaptor).

Plugging an iPad or iPhone into the USB port of a computer allows you to transfer photos and other media from the device to your computer, perform a backup of the device to your computer, or 'sync' media from your computer to your iPhone/iPad.

The charging capacities of the iPad and iPhone adaptors differ – for example, iPad's is 10W (or 12W for iPad Pro), iPhone's is 5W.

An iPad charger can be used to charge an iPhone, and vice versa. Charging an iPad with an iPhone power adaptor will take longer than with the iPad's standard adaptor.

Discovering The Sleep/Wake Switch

One button on your iPad/iPhone is used to put your device to 'sleep', 'wake' it up and do a number of other things – where these other things depend on the type of iPad / iPhone you have.

This button is known as the **Sleep/Wake Switch**. On iPads, this switch is on the top right when your device is in 'portrait' orientation (indicated in below images).

On iPhones, the Sleep Switch is on the right side of the iPhone.

Putting your device to 'sleep' and 'waking' it again

If your device is currently 'awake' (i.e. something is showing on the screen), **one quick press of the Sleep/Wake switch** will put your iPhone or iPad into a **'standby' (sleeping) mode** (the screen will go black).

While it is asleep, your device consumes very little power but is still ready to wake up for calls and alerts (notifications).

If your device is currently asleep (i.e. the screen is black), **one quick press of the Sleep/Wake switch** will wake it up and show your 'Lock Screen' (which we will describe a bit later).

If your device has a Home button, press that button to wake up your device. For devices without a Home button, simply tap the screen to wake the device. (If this tap of the screen doesn't work, there is a Setting that is turned off - **Settings -> Accessibility -> Touch -> Tap to Wake.**)

Generally, just put your device to sleep when not using it, rather than turning it off completely (described next). We will also look later at how you set your device to automatically go to sleep after a period of inactivity.

Some iPad covers are magnetic and can perform sleep/wake functions when opened and closed. If your iPad does this, you may rarely need use the **Sleep/Wake Switch** for this purpose.

Discovering The
Sleep/Wake Switch

Using the Sleep/Wake switch to silence a call

A handy tip for iPhone users is that you can use the Sleep Switch to quickly **silence a ringing iPhone**. This does also apply to the iPad, although tends to be something you need more on the iPhone than the iPad.

Press Sleep Switch <u>once</u> when the device is ringing (just a quick press).

Press twice
quickly to
silence &
send call to
Voicemail

This will silence the ringing, but the iPhone may still vibrate if it has been set up to vibrate on calls.

Press the Sleep Switch twice quickly in succession when it is ringing to stop both the ringing and the vibration.

This will send the phone call straight to your Voicemail (assuming this is set up).

I use the double-press of the Sleep Switch on a very regular basis, when I can't take a call during an appointment or class!

Powering Your Device
On and Off

To turn your iPad or iPhone off

On iPhones and iPads that have a Home Button: Hold down the **Sleep Switch** for about **3 seconds**, then **'Slide to Power Off'** to confirm that you wish to turn off the device (i.e. put your finger on the circle at the top and slide to the right).

On devices that don't have a Home Button (iPhone X series, 11, 12, 13, 14 and some newer iPads): Press and hold the **Sleep** button and either **Volume** button at the same time.

If you didn't mean to turn your device off, just tap the ⓧ at the bottom to continue working on your iPad or iPhone. You will be required to first enter the device's passcode (if you have set one).

Once it is turned off, your device will not consume any power or wake for alerts and notifications – it is **completely OFF**.

To turn your iPad or iPhone back on

Hold down the **Sleep switch** for about **2-3 seconds**. An Apple symbol will pop up to show it is turning back on. Be patient – sometimes it takes a bit of time for this startup to complete.

When your device 'wakes up' or completes its powering up, the first screen that shows will be shown your '**Lock Screen**'.

We will describe this special screen in more detail shortly.

Interacting with your iPhone or iPad's screen

On your iPad and iPhone, your finger is all-powerful and controls everything you do on your device. It is the equivalent of your mouse on a computer - but is a lot more powerful than a mouse.

Here are the main standard gestures:

* **Tap** – to open an app or select something. Just a **gentle tap** using the <u>pad</u> of your finger (or a Stylus). Don't touch and hold, as this is a different gesture. Don't use your fingernail – it must be the pad of your finger.

* **Touch and hold** – in certain places, touching and holding on a spot will bring up some options or cause something to happen. An example of this is the space bar on the keyboard – touch and hold (without moving your finger) on the spacebar to change the keyboard to a trackpad, then drag your finger around the trackpad to move the cursor around.

* **Drag** – touch the screen then (without lifting it) move your finger around the screen - usually to move something from one place to another, to re-position the screen, or to move up and down (or left to right) through a list.

* **Swipe** – to move left or right between screens

* **Flick** – fast version of a swipe (up and down), to quickly move a list up and down (touch to stop scrolling)

* **Pinch & spread** – zoom in and out (e.g. on a photo or in the Maps app). Touch the screen with two fingers and then drag them outwards or inwards.

* **Two finger tap** – to zoom out on Maps.

* **Single finger double tap** – to zoom in on Maps or on a web page in Safari (two taps in quick succession). In Safari, double tap again with single finger to reverse the zoom

* **Force Touch** – Some iPhones have another finger gesture called **Force Touch.** Touch and press on an App icon on the Home Screen to see a set of options for that app – providing quick access to features of the app. **Force Touch** also works in various apps. (Note. Force Touch was phased out in more recent iPhone models, and the Touch and Hold gesture replaces it.)

Your device and flying

You are usually asked to **switch off electronic device/s** (such as your iPad & iPhone) for plane takeoff and landing.

You will also be asked to first put all electronic devices into **Aeroplane Mode** for the entire flight.

When you turn on Aeroplane Mode, the device it is on 'radio silence'. It will be disconnected from any phone network, Internet or Bluetooth services. While in this mode, you can still play games, read books, listen to music stored on your device and more. You can also re-connect to Wi-Fi and Bluetooth while in Aeroplane mode.

To turn on Aeroplane Mode on your iPhone and iPad...

On your Home Screen, tap on the **Settings** app.
Slide **Aeroplane Mode** (the top option) to 'On' so that it is green

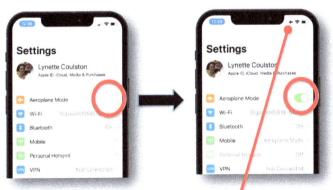

An aeroplane symbol ✈ appears at the top of the screen – top left on devices with a Home button, top right on those without (as shown in example above right). This shows that you are in Aeroplane Mode.

Slide **Aeroplane Mode** to 'Off' (no longer green) to re-connect once you have landed.

You can also easily turn Aeroplane Mode on and off from your **Control Centre**, which we cover later on in this guide.

The Lock Screen

When your iPhone or iPad is 'woken up' or 'turned on', the first screen that appears will be the **Lock Screen**.

The purpose of the Lock Screen is to keep your device secure from unauthorized access, and to prevent inadvertent actions caused by touches on the screen – pocket calling is one example of this!

Unlocking the iPad and iPhone

To unlock a device that has a Home Button, you can simply **press the Home Button**. You will then be prompted to enter your device passcode (if it has one).

If you have a Home Button with the fingerprint sensor
AND you have set up your device to recognise one or more of your fingerprints (we'll cover this a bit later)

• Pressing the **Home Button** with one of these fingers will immediately unlock and open your device.

• Just **holding your finger on the sensor without pressing** will unlock the device but leave you on the Lock Screen (so that you can access the other features of the Lock screen).

If your device supports Face ID and you have set this up, simply looking at your device will unlock your device so that you can access information on the Lock Screen (or allow you to go to your Home Screen).

If you are not using a fingerprint or **Face ID** to unlock the device (or your fingerprint/face is not recognised),

• Pressing the **Home Button** on the **Lock Screen** will (usually) give you a screen that requires entry of your device's Passcode to open your device.

We'll talk more about setting up a device Passcode and fingerprints (or Face ID) later – and about how you can (if no fingerprint/face is recorded) delay how soon after 'sleeping' your device needs you to re-enter the passcode.

Discovering The
Sleep/Wake Switch

The lock screen can also provide some other key information and functions

- New notifications appear in the middle
- See other previous Notifications (applies when time is showing on lock screen) - *Drag upwards slightly from the middle of the screen*
- Fast access to your **Camera** - *Swipe from right to left* or (for iPhone only) *touch and hold on the camera symbol at bottom right of the screen*
- Access to **Search and Siri Suggestions** - *Drag down from centre of screen)*
- Access to **Control Centre** – *Swipe up from below bottom of screen* for iPhones with a Home Button OR *Swipe down from top right corner* on all iPads and on iPhones using FaceID

    These extra Lock Screen functions (and how to control them) are covered in the sections on Notifications and Control Centre later in this guide.

Introducing Customised Lock Screens

New in iOS 16 (iPhone only). With the arrival of iOS 16, the Lock Screen of the iPhone can be customised in several ways.

You can now add Widgets to the Home screen, and you can set up multiple Home Screens, each with different wallpapers (background image), widgets, and look.

We cover this new feature in more detail later in this guide.

Introducing Settings

The **Settings** App on your iPad and iPhone is where you set up and choose how your iPad or iPhone works for you. We will refer to **Settings** frequently in iTandCoffee guides.

You will find yourself visiting **Settings** on a regular basis for things like.

- connecting to Wi/Fi

- putting your device in **Aeroplane Mode** when flying

- adjusting your **Mail, Contacts and Calendars** settings

- changing the sounds of your rings and alerts

- changing your preferences for things like font size, sort orders, etc.

- checking your iPad's or iPhone's storage usage

- turning your 'Personal Hotspot' on and off

- and much more!

Don't be afraid to explore **Settings** – there are so many things you can set up and change to make your device work the way you want it to!

This guide will have a look at a few areas of Settings that are not covered in other iTandCoffee guides. In this section, we take a quick look at the different categories of settings that are available.

Introducing Settings

Navigating Settings

On your iPad, the main **Settings** options and categories are listed on the left.

On your iPhone, these main settings options take up the whole screen.

Touch on particular Settings item to see configuration and preference options that are available for this item.

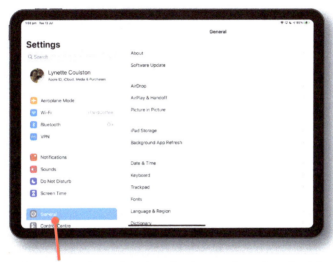

For example, the **General** set of settings has been selected on the left on the above iPad screen, showing the various General options on the right.

For some of the **Settings** shown for the item you have selected, you will be able to just touch on the Setting to 'tick' it to select it; or you will be able to slide its 'slider' to turn it on or off (where 'on' is represented by left side showing green).

For many main **Settings** options, there is more than one 'level' of preferences, settings or information associated with that main option.

Wherever there are further 'choices' to make for a particular option/setting, there will be a > symbol on the right-hand side of that option. Tap on the option to see the 'sub-options'.

Introducing Settings

An example of navigating Settings

Let's look at what I mean by this.

In the example below, I have touched on the **General** option on the left. Looking at **About** on the right, the > on the right indicates that **About** has some further options. Tap > to see these options

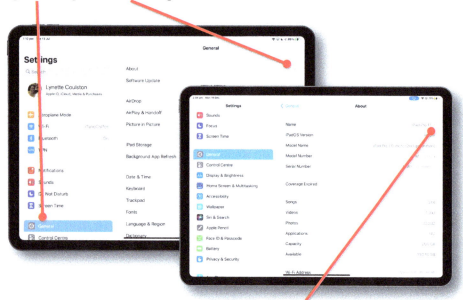

The > next to **Name** indicates that there are some choices I can make for that Setting.

Then, **to go back** a level, tap the arrow symbol at top left (in this case it says < About) at the top left – this will take me back to the full set of **About** settings.

From the About settings, I can then choose the < General option at top left to go back to the full set of **General** settings.

On an iPad: Alternatively, when I was in the **Name** setting screen on my iPad, I could have just touched on **General** in the left sidebar to go straight back to the main **General** Settings screen.

Introducing Settings

This method of navigating the different 'levels' within apps is common across most Apps on your iPad and iPhone.

Whenever you wish to go 'back' to the previous screen 'level', look for the blue word with < at the top left. (Sometimes there is just the < with no word.) Touch this to move back.

On your iPhone, you can also swipe across the screen from left to right to go back a level.

A quick look at Settings

Let's look at the main sections of **Settings**. You will find that some of the more frequently used **Settings** appear in the main menu on the **Settings** list, while others are found under broader categories of **Settings**.

At the very top of **Settings** is your name. Tapping on this provides access to details of your Apple ID (your account with Apple), your iCloud setup, your Media and Purchases setup, Find My setup, Family Sharing setup, and more. We look at this in more detail in the **'The Comprehensive Guide to iCloud'** user guide.

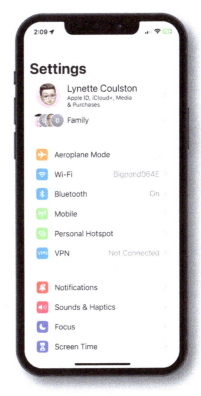

The second section of **Settings** looks after preferences and settings to do with connectivity to the Internet, Wi-Fi, phone service (for iPhones), and to other devices.

We will look at the 'Bluetooth' setting shortly later in this guide. Other settings listed here are covered in other guides.

The next group of options allows you to control alerts and notifications, your **Notifications**, **Sounds**, and your **Focus** settings (described in more detail later).

This section also includes the **Screen Time** option, which helps you manage your own, and your child's, device usage and set parental controls. We cover this set of settings in a separate guide, called **Keeping your Children Safe on the iPad, iPhone & iPod Touch**.

Introducing Settings

The **fourth section** covers a variety of areas that control your iPad's/iPhone's operation, security and privacy.

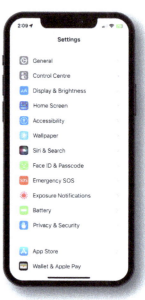

Touch ID & Passcode or **Face ID & Passcode** if the device does not have Touch ID) is where your passcode and its settings can be established. (We look at this a bit later.)

You can determine what functions/symbols appear in your Control Centre (we cover this later), control the brightness of the screen, the size of text on the screen, your sounds, Siri, see where your battery is being used most, and control what private information can be used by the device's apps and functions.

You can also set up something called **Emergency SOS** so that you can quickly contact emergency services if you are in trouble, as well as quickly disabling your Touch ID/Face ID if you need.

The **fifth section** shows your Apps Store setup and includes the settings relating to your Wallet app and Apple Pay.

The **sixth section** allows the setup of accounts and options for many other standard apps.

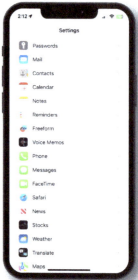

Passwords is where you can view all the passwords that have been 'remembered' by your device. These may also sync to your other Apple devices using something called Keychain.

Mail, Contacts, Calendars, Notes and **Reminders** options allow you to connect the device to the relevant accounts for managing this data (eg. Gmail, iCloud, Outlook, Exchange etc) and establish the various settings for these apps, including the default account that should apply for each. We look at these settings in separate guides about each of these apps.

Set a password that will apply when you 'lock' your **Notes** and choose their sort order and a 'note template'.

Sign into with your Apple ID for **Facetime** and **Messages** – making sure to use your own Apple ID, not a shared family Apple ID - and define various settings for other apps.

Introducing Settings

For **Safari,** there are a number of settings worth exploring, including controls over popups, cookies and tracking.

It is well worth tapping on each option in this set to see what options are available.

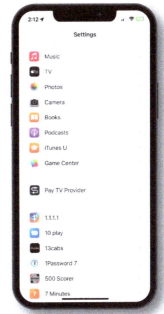

The next group has settings for the various 'entertainment' apps on your iPad and iPhone, as well as settings for your **Camera** and **Photo** apps.

The final section lists the settings options that apply to the Apps that you have downloaded to your device from The App Store.

Some will just show the version of the app you are running and not much more.

Others will give you further preferences and settings that customise your version of the app.

We'll cover a few important options in **Settings** later in this guide. Other Settings are covered in guides about individual Apps and specialist topics.

Getting online!
Joining a Wi-Fi Network

To access the internet using an iPad or iPhone, the device must be connected to either a Wi-Fi network or a Mobile Data network.

(Refer **Terminology** section at start for more information about these terms.)

Wi-Fi Options in Settings

Here is how to connect to a nearby Wi-Fi network so that you can access the internet using that network.

- In **Settings** app again, tap the word **Wi-Fi**

- **Wi-Fi** must be **On** (green) - slide the dot to right if it is not green

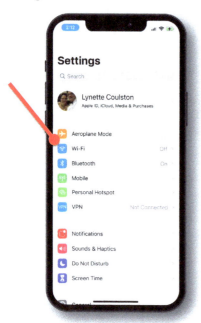

- You will see a list of available Wi-Fi networks that your device can 'see' in the area surrounding you. Only those Wi-Fi networks that are within about 20-50 metres will show. So, don't expect to see your home Wi-Fi network name there if you are not at home.

- You may find that your device has automatically joined a network that it has 'remembered'.

Getting online!
Joining a Wi-Fi Network

- If not, tap the name of the network you wish to join. Make sure to **tap on the name**, <u>not</u> the ⓘ

- You will be asked to type in the Password for that network.

- Enter the password you have been provided, then choose Join (top right or on the Keyboard).

Once you have successfully joined the selected Wi-Fi network, a tick will show on the left of the Network Name.

You will also notice the Wi-Fi symbol appears at top of the screen (top left on devices with a Home Button, top right on those without).

This shows you are now connected to Wi-Fi.

Your device will then 'remember' this Wi-Fi network.
This means that, whenever you are 'in range' of the network (and if your Wi-Fi is enabled), your device will automatically connect to it, using this network in preference to your Mobile Data service (for cases where you have a device with a SIM card and a connected service).

An important thing to note is that the Wi-Fi symbol and tick are showing whether you have a connection to the Wi-Fi network, to the router.

This doesn't necessarily mean that you have internet.

So, if you are finding that you can't connect to something, that you don't seem to be 'online' even though you see the Wi-Fi symbol, always check that your router and modem are working and connected to the internet.

A restart of the router and/or modem may be required rule out a problem there. If you still can't connect to the internet, check if your Internet Service Provider is suffering an outage.

If your device refuses to join a 'known' network

If ever your device has a problem connecting to a Wi-Fi network that it has previously successfully joined, it may be that the network password or some other aspect of its configuration has changed.

Getting online!
Joining a Wi-Fi Network

As a result, you will need to get your device to 'forget' what it already knew about the network and re-connect.

To reconnect to the network, tap the symbol ⓘ on the right of the network name, then choose the option to **Forget This Network**.

Once you have done that, follow the steps described earlier to re-join the network – i.e. re-select the network from the list of available networks, and re-join by typing in the current network password.

If your device keeps joining a particular network in preference to another

On occasion, your device can 'remember' too many networks – and can automatically join a network that you don't want it to join.

An example is, here in Australia, that a device may connect to Telstra Air instead of your home Wi-Fi. This can mean that, even though your Wi-Fi shows a connection, you are not able to get internet.

Another example may be where you have a printer that provides its own Wi-Fi network for printing, but your device seems to join that in preference to your home Wi-Fi.

In this case you don't want to 'forget' the other network – you just don't want it to join the network automatically.

Tap the ⓘ symbol on the right of each nearby network to see and manage the option to enable or disable something called **Auto-Join**.

For any network that you want to choose to manually join (instead of automatically joining), turn the **Auto-Join** switch to off (not green).

Join a Wi-Fi Network from Control Centre

Another way of connecting to a Wi-Fi network is from your Control Centre. We will look at this later in this guide.

Getting online!
Joining a Wi-Fi Network

Look up the Wi-Fi Password

New in iOS/iPadOS 16. You can now look up the Password associated with your device's current Wi-Fi network. This can be very handy in certain situations, where you need to be able to provide the password to someone or to some device.

You must be currently connected to the relevant network for this to work.

Tap on the ⓘ symbol on the right of the ticked Wi-Fi network. You will see there is no a **Password** field under the **Auto-Join** option. Tap the dots, then authenticate with your Face ID, Touch ID or Passcode to show the network's Password. You will see the option to Copy this password (if needed).

A Quick Look at Home Screens

Home Screens are the main screens on your iPhone and iPad. Your Home Screens show your **Apps**.

When you first get your iPad or iPhone, the Home Screen will show several standard Apps that Apple has given you.

Add more Apps to your device by visiting the **App Store**, where you can download free Apps, or purchase 'paid' Apps.

When you get Apps from the App Store, they are usually added to one of your Home Screens – in the next available spot on the second or subsequent Home Screen.

If that doesn't happen, then it may be that your newly downloaded apps go straight into and area called the App Library (we describe this later). This is due to a particular setting in **Settings -> Home Screen,** where the option **App Library Only** has been chosen.

The more Apps you download/buy, the more Home Screens you may have. Later in this guide, we look at how you can move your Apps around within a Home Screen, and between Home Screens. We will also talk about the new (since iOS 15) **App Library**, showing all the apps that you have on your device.

To move between Home Screens, swipe across the screen with one finger – right to left to move to the next screen, left to right to go back a screen.

The dots near the bottom of each Home Screen show how many Home Screens there are, and which one you are currently viewing.

Opening an App

Open an App with a Tap

As mentioned above, your Home Screen shows a set of icons representing the Apps that you have on your device.

To open any app, simply tap the app.

As mentioned earlier, make sure when you tap that you use the pad of your finger – not your fingernail.

Most apps will return you to the place where you left off when they open.

For example, if you were in the middle of writing an email in the Mail app, then jumped out of the Mail app, when you return to the Mail app, that draft email will be the first thing you see.

If you have been using the Safari app to look at a particular web page, the next time you tap Safari, that same page will show.

Or touch and hold on an App to see some special options

There are also some handy 'shortcuts' available when opening an app, shortcuts that allow you to jump straight to a particular feature of the app.

These options are presented when you 'touch and hold' on an app on the Home Screen. A context-sensitive menu will appear, allowing you to choose (by tapping) one of the options presented.

Below are just some examples below for the Photos, Notes, Mail and Contacts apps.

If you don't want to choose any of the options presented, simply tap elsewhere on the screen to close that special menu and see your Home Screen again.

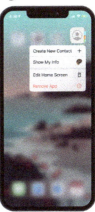

Returning to the Home Screen

On devices without a Home Button

Whenever you want to switch from one App to another (or just exit an App), put your finger on the line at the bottom of the screen, and **swipe upwards** a little. It only needs to be a gentle flick upwards.

On Devices with a Home Button

The main function of the **Home Button** is to take you back to the Home Screen from whichever App you are in.

Home Button

Whenever you want to switch from one App to another (or just exit an App), press the **Home Button** to go back to the **Home Screen**.

Only a quick press is required – if you press for a longer period, you will cause something quite different to happen (which we will cover shortly).

For all devices

Think of the **Swipe Up** or **Home Button** press as your 'Quit' or 'Escape' (if you come from the computer world), to get out of whatever App or feature you are currently in and return to your Home Screen – to 'go home'.

The Dock

At the bottom of your iPad or iPhone's Home Screen, you will see a row of apps on a bar. This area is called **the Dock** and is where you choose to put your most frequently used apps.

The Dock is always visible from any of your Home Screens, giving you easy access to your most used apps. We will look later at how to move apps into and out of the Dock (and between Home Screens).

On the iPhone, the Dock can only hold 4 apps.

However, the **iPad's** Dock can hold lots more apps.

On the biggest iPad, the Dock can hold 15 apps. The smaller iPads can hold up to 11 apps.

The iPad dock now also shows the most recently used apps on the right-hand side, making it easier to switch between apps you have been using recently. These recently used apps are separated from the other Dock apps by a faint grey vertical line.

(If you don't want to see this separate section for 'recently used' apps, go to **Settings -> Home Screen & Multitasking** and disable the **Show Suggested and Recent Apps in Dock** setting.)

Another great feature on the iPad is the ability to access this Dock while you are using any App – simply by dragging slightly up from below the bottom of the screen.

In the example on the right, I have brought up the **Dock** while in the **Notes** App, allowing me to switch to any of the apps in the Dock – or to view 2 screens at once using Slide Over or 'Split Screen' view (described later in this guide).

What's going on with my screen?

New users of the iPad and iPhone frequently find themselves viewing screens that they are not familiar with, and are often left wondering what to do, and how to get out of them.

Basic Rule for Getting Back to Home Screen

There is a basic rule that will work in the majority of cases ...

To get out of whatever app or mode/screen you have accidentally activated,

- swipe up from the bottom (if you don't have a Home Button) or

- press of the Home button (if you do have a Home Button).

We'll look now at some things that might happen on your iPad or iPhone that may leave you feeling a bit lost!

My screen has changed and has some messages on it.

If your screen shows your lock screen background and something like the screen below, this appeared because you **swiped down from <u>above</u> the top of the screen** (anywhere from top left to top middle).

This is called the **Notification Centre** (covered a bit later) and can be very useful.

But if you don't want it,

- swipe up from the bottom of the screen to close it (if you don't have a Home Button) or

- press the Home Button (if you have one).

What's going on with my screen?

My screen has a heap of boxes and symbols on it

If your Home Screen seems to be 'taken over' with boxes and symbols, don't worry.

You have accidentally activated a feature called the **Control Centre** by

- swiping upwards from below the bottom of the screen on an iPhone with a Home button or

- by swiping downwards from the top right of the screen on the iPad or an iPhone that doesn't have a Home Button.

Here's how to get out of this screen:

- just tap the screen somewhere (not on the icons shown though) to make it go away OR

- swipe up from the bottom of the screen to close it (if you don't have a Home Button) OR

- press the Home Button (if you have one).

(See later in this guide for more on the **Control Centre**.)

What's going on with my screen?

I have a screen all sorts of apps and boxes on it

If your screen looks something like that below, you have **swiped left to right** from your **first Home Screen** and activated something called the **Today View**. (We describe this later in the guide, in the section on Notifications.)

This view provides all sorts of handy information about what's on, what's happening, and mini-apps called 'Widgets' – and you get to choose what you see here.

But if you don't want it,

- swipe up from the bottom of the screen to close it (if you don't have a Home Button) or

- press the Home Button (if you have one).

My screen has a 'Search' bar and some apps

If your Home Screen has a 'Search' bar on the screen (either at the top or in the middle) and shows the keyboard at the bottom (and perhaps has some other information listed that covers up the iPhone Home Screen), you have activated a feature called **Spotlight Search** (which is covered a bit later in this guide)

Spotlight Search is activated by **dragging downwards from the centre of the Home Screen**.

But if you don't want it,

What's going on with my screen?

- swipe up from the bottom of the screen to close it (if you don't have a Home Button or

- press the Home Button (if you have one).

My Apps have started wiggling!

If the apps on your Home Screen have started **wiggling**, with some of them perhaps showing an **x** at the top left ...

You have activated the '**Edit Mode'** for your Apps by holding your finger on one of the Apps for a few seconds or so, or by holding on a vacant area of the screen for a second or so.

This mode allows you to delete apps, move apps around, group apps, add 'widgets' to your Home Screen, and more.

We cover this 'Wiggle Mode'/'Edit Mode' a bit later in this guide.

If you want to stop the Wiggle

- tap **Done** at the top right or

- swipe up from the bottom of the screen to close it (if you don't have a Home Button) or

- press the Home Button (if you have one).

What's going on with my screen?

My screen has a strange coloured circle on it

If your screen shows a strange circle/orb at the bottom, you have activated the **Siri** (your device's built-in personal assistant) function by

- holding the Home Button (assuming you have one!) for longer than a second.

- holding the sleep/wake switch for about second (if your device doesn't have a Home Button)

- saying something that sounds like 'Hey Siri'.

Siri is waiting for you to give it a command.

For example, you could say "Text my husband I will be home by 6" to send the message "I will be home by 6" to your husband.

We talk a bit about Siri later in this guide.

If you want to make the Siri symbol go away,

- swipe up from the bottom of the screen to close it (if you don't have a Home Button or

- press the Home Button (if you have one)

- wait few seconds and it will disappear.

Where is my keyboard?

A common question asked by those who are new to the iPad and iPhone is '**Where is my keyboard?**' and '**Why can't I see my keyboard?**'.

Well, we have another basic rule here about the on-screen keyboard ...

Your keyboard will only appear when it is required.

For your keyboard to appear, you must have touched somewhere that requires you to type something. Examples include:

- touching on a Search field;

- creating something that needs some information entered e.g. writing a new email, replying to an email;

- creating a new Note or document or modifying an existing Note or document.

If you don't see your keyboard, have a think about where you are and what you are looking at. (Of course, if you have a separate physical keyboard for your iPad, you won't see the on-screen keyboard.)

Look at where your 'cursor' is positioned (to line that shows your text position). Have you touched on a field requiring entry, or started a new message or note and tapped a place that requires some text?

Tap on the screen in the spot where you need to type something, and the on-screen keyboard should magically appear (assuming again you don't have a physical keyboard).

When you use a separate physical keyboard

If you are using a separate physical keyboard with your iPad or iPhone, you will not necessarily see an on-screen keyboard.

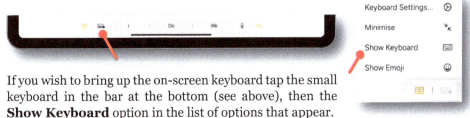

If you wish to bring up the on-screen keyboard tap the small keyboard in the bar at the bottom (see above), then the **Show Keyboard** option in the list of options that appear.

My screen doesn't give me any options!

Why are there no options?

The apps on your iPad and iPhone are designed to make the most of the beautiful screens on your devices, so you will often find that your screen is taken up with a beautiful image, a book, or some other content – but does not seem to provide any options or menus to get out of what you are viewing or do anything with the content of your screen, while staying in the App.

For example, the screen on the right shows that I am reading one of the iTandCoffee books in Apple's Books app.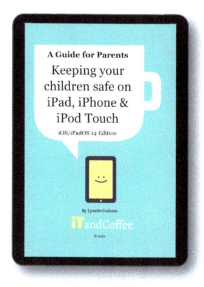

This book is taking up the full screen and shows no options at the top or bottom.

So, how do I get back to my list of books, or see the other available Books options – for example, if I wanted to get out of this book and return to my full 'Library' of books?

Showing app's options

Just tap the middle of the screen to reveal the options bar at the top (and maybe the bottom).

As you can see in the image on the right, there are now options available for me at the top, plus a 'browse bar' along the bottom.

This general rule applies in many apps that show content in full screen mode.

Hiding app's options again

Tap on the middle of the screen again to make the options disappear and return to 'full screen' mode.

Auto-Locking your iPhone and iPad

When you are not using your iPad or iPhone, it should be in 'Lock' mode. This means that the **Lock Screen** is showing (as described earlier in this guide).

It is a good idea to make use of the automatic locking feature of your device – not only to prevent 'pocket-dialing' by your iPhone, but to also stop your device's battery going flat quickly. The display being on is one of the biggest drains on the battery.

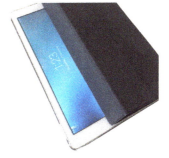

Many iPads have magnetic covers that lock the iPad when the cover is closed.

However, it is still important to set up the **Auto-lock** feature so that the device locks when the cover is left off for any period of time (on iPad), or when the iPhone/iPad is not being used.

You can turn on and adjust the **Auto-lock** feature in **Settings**

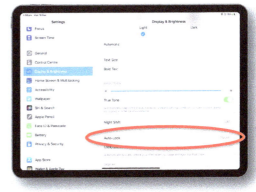

- Look for **Settings -> Display & Brightness** in the main Settings list, and the option **Auto-lock**.

- If this is set to 'Never', then your device will not automatically lock.

- Touch on **Auto-lock**, then, from the list of intervals presented to you, tap to select the time period after which the device should lock.

- For iPhone especially, it is best to make this interval not too long – again, to prevent 'pocket-dialling' or 'bag calling' someone by accident, but also and as a security precaution.

If your iPhone goes into 'Low Power Mode' due to a battery level of less than 20%, the Auto-Lock setting will automatically change to 30 seconds and cannot be changed until 'Low Power Mode' is turned off again (when the battery is sufficiently charged or when you manually turn of 'Low Power Mode' in **Settings -> Battery**, or from Command Centre, which we will cover soon).

Introducing some of the Standard Apps

Your iPad and iPhone come with many standard apps. Here is a brief description of many of the main apps.

Settings: Settings (which we had a quick look at earlier) is the place to check on and customise the way you want your iDevice to operate. It's where you go to connect to email accounts and define various settings and preferences. Settings is your friend, so don't be afraid of this App!

Safari: The Safari app is a 'web browser', allowing you to 'surf' the Internet and save bookmarks of favourite sites. This is where you perform your Google searches, look up recipes, research holiday destinations, do your banking online, and so much more!

Mail: The Mail app gives you easy access to all the email accounts that you use. You see a list of your emails and read them by touching on them. Various standard mailboxes are provided (Inbox, Sent, Trash, etc.) and, for some types of mail account, you can also set up your own set of mailboxes for filing and organizing your mail.

Messages: The Messages App allows you to send SMS's (the green speech bubbles) and SMS-style messages called iMessages (where iMessages use the internet instead of your SMS allowance – the blue speech bubbles). Your communications with other people are shown as friendly 'conversations' in speech bubbles.

Contacts: Contacts is your address book on your iPad and iPhone. It allows you to enter contact information (email address, phone numbers, address) for friends, family, and colleagues. The other Apple Apps on your iPad and iPhone can then use the information stored in your Contacts to 'auto-fill' people's details when you just enter their name. If you record birthdates of friends and family in your Contacts, they will automatically appear in your Calendar, and you can be reminded in advance! If you record street addresses in Contacts, you can ask Siri to give you directions to where your contact resides (or works).

Phone: The Phone app allows you to make and receive calls, view recent callers, set up Favourite people, and check your voicemail. It also includes a Contacts option (same features as in the Contacts apps) to access all your contacts from within the Phone app.

Introducing some of the Standard Apps

Camera: The Camera app allows you to take photos and videos using your iPad or iPhone. The cameras on newer iPhones and iPads are excellent, and have features like portrait mode, live mode, telephoto and more.

Photos: The photos App is where you can view the photos you have taken using your iPad or iPhone, or saved to your device from email, messages, the internet and your digital camera. Organise pictures into albums, share photos with others, use a photo as your Lock Screen or Home Screen 'wallpaper' (i.e. background), and assign photos to people in the Contacts App. Run slideshows of your photos or just swipe through full-screen views of your photos. Through iCloud, you manage your photos from any of your devices – with albums, edits, facial recognition and more sync'ing between your devices.

Music: This app allows you to listen to music in your music library, Apple Radio, or Apple Music (if you are a subscriber). Create playlists of your favourite music!
New Sing feature in Music:
iOS/iPadOS 16.2 has brought the 'Sing' feature to the Music app – where you can use the Music app for Karaoke.

Calendar: Calendar provides you with an electronic diary and calendar. It allows you to set up appointments, engagements and events – and the best thing is that it can provide alerts to remind you about them. And you can share a calendar with others.

Reminders: Record your To-Do list, schedule tasks and even create reminders that alert you when you arrive at a particular place. Reminders can be recurring and are so easy to create using Siri.

Notes: This wonderful app allows recording of anything! For example shopping lists, a list of books or movies you have been recommended, pieces of information that you want to quickly record and access easily. You can even hand-write and draw your Notes, add photos, scan documents, and save web links here. Notes can be organized into a Folder/Sub-Folder structure, Tags can be used to further organize Notes, Notes can be shared, and more.

Maps: Find directions from one place to another by car, foot, or public transportation, view maps, zoom in and out. Now you can toss out that street directory!

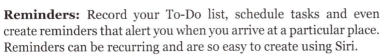

Introducing some of the Standard Apps

TV: This media player plays movies and TV programs that are stored on your iPad or iPhone, or videos that you have rented. (This app used to be the **Videos** app before iOS 11.) The TV app also shows what's on from the various catch-up TV and subscription services (for example, from ABC iView, TenPlay, Netflix, Stan, Binge, etc.).

iTunes Store: This App allows you to purchase music, movies, TV shows, and ringtones. You can download these directly to your iPad and iPhone, or 'stream' them without downloading.

Podcasts: Find a wealth of free (and, more recently, paid) content in Podcasts – audio and video shows that have been recorded from radio, TV and by other content providers. It's really worth exploring.

App Store: The App Store allows you to buy and download all sorts of Apps (applications). Categories include games, tools, magazines, utilities, special interest, and so much more. So much is free!

FaceTime: The FaceTime app allows you the make a video call, involving one or more people. It is similar to Zoom, Skype, etc., and very easy to use. You can also use FaceTime audio – which is like making a phone call without needing a phone service, using the internet instead! This is great when you are travelling or have family and friends living far away. With iOS/iPadOS 16, Facetime call participants don't have to Apple users, calls can be pre-arranged, and a new feature called SharePlay is included or sharing your screen with others on the call.

Books: The Books App (previously named iBooks) allows you to buy and download books and audiobooks, to read or listen to on your iPad or iPhone. You can sample books before you buy. Books also provides a place to store PDFs. Use Collections to categorise your content.

Files: This used to be the iCloud Drive app before iOS 11. Files provides you somewhere to store all your files – your PDFs, Word and Excel documents, and various other files that you need to store on your iPad or iPhone. Set up folders within this area and sync your files with your other devices. Files can also integrate your other Cloud services like OneDrive and Dropbox.

Introducing some of the Standard Apps

Voice Memo: If you ever need to record some audio on your iPhone or iPad, the Voice Memo app will perform this function.

Wallet: Wallet is where you set up something called Apple Pay by adding your credit card/s. Wallet will scan your card, and then allow you to use your iPhone to pay for goods using this credit card. It also allows you to store 'virtual' versions of boarding passes, tickets, reward cards, hotel bookings, gift cards, vouchers, and more.

Health: Collect health data from your Apple Watch (if you have one) and track your steps and activity. Make sure you fill out your Medical ID and Emergency Contacts in the Health app so that emergency services can access vital information from your iPhone.

Find My: Find My helps you locate and protect your Apple device if it's ever lost or stolen. To use it, your device must be signed in to iCloud. When needed, you can use this app to locate your missing device, play a sound (even if it is muted), register it as 'lost' and more. Find My also shows details of any family members and friends who have shared their location with you – allowing you to help locate their devices (and them) as well if needed.

News: News collects all the stories you want to read from publications around the world. You can also 'curate' articles on a variety of topics. If you subscribe to Apple's premium News+ service, you can access a range of subscriber-only publications.

Measure: The Measure app allows you to measure a object or surface using your iPhone or iPad or quickly view a person's height. On the iPhone, the Measure app also includes a 'level' function – so that you can place your iPhone on a surface to check if it is level.

Pages, Numbers Keynote: These apps are Apple's equivalent of the Microsoft Office suite of Word, Excel and PowerPoint. **Pages** allows you to create documents, **Numbers** allows creation of spreadsheets, and **Keynote** is for presentations. If you are not particularly skilled in the Microsoft suite, it is worth using this set of **free** Apple apps – instead of paying extra money for Microsoft.

Other standard apps include Watch, Weather, Stocks, Phone, Compass and Tips.
New Freeform App
Also new in iOS/iPadOS 16 is the **Freefrom App**, for brainstorming, diagramming, collaborating. We'll leave you to explore those ones on your own.

Exploring Control Centre

What is Control Centre?

The **Control Centre** is a great feature that provides quick access to commonly used settings, features, and apps.

Access **Control Centre** from anywhere —the Lock Screen*, the Home Screen or from within Apps*. (*See later for how you can block access to Control Centre from the Lock screen, and from within apps.)

How to access Control Centre

To access **Control Centre**,

- On iPads, and on iPhones without a Home Button, **drag down from the top right** of the screen.
- On iPhones with a home button, **drag up from <u>below the bottom</u>** of the screen.

Control Centre on iPad

Control Centre on iPhone

How to close Control Centre

To close **Control Centre** or go back a level

- On all devices tap a vacant area of the screen
- On iPhones without a Home Button, swipe up from the bottom of the screen
- On iPhones with a Home Button, swipe down from the top of the screen or press the Home Button.

Exploring Control Centre

Using Control Centre

The first section of controls offers a quick way turning off and on all the connectivity settings for Wi-Fi, Bluetooth, Mobile Data, Personal Hotspot, and Airdrop.

The Personal Hotspot and Airdrop settings are not visible at first in Control Centre. **Touch and hold** on the first section of controls to see the full set and to see connection information.

Touch and hold also shows further options or a pop-up screen for the following symbols/areas: media controls, brightness control, volume control, screen mirroring, torch, timer, calculator and camera. Just touch and hold to see what is 'behind' each symbol/area. Let's look now at the meaning of the different symbols.

	Aeroplane Mode	Turn **Aeroplane Mode** on or off. Circle is orange when Aeroplane mode is on. (See earlier in guide for more.)
	Wi-Fi	**Temporarily** turn off <u>nearby</u> **Wi-Fi** <u>until tomorrow</u>. Circle is white when Wi-Fi is off.
		It is important to note that this will not completely turn off Wi-Fi – to do this, visit **Settings -> Wi-Fi.**
	Mobile Data	Turn **Mobile Data** (also known as Cellular Data) off and on. Circle turns grey when off – mobile data will stay off until you turn it back on.
	Bluetooth	**Temporarily** turn off Bluetooth <u>until tomorrow</u>. Circle is white when Bluetooth is off, blue when on. It is important to note that this will not completely turn off Bluetooth – to do this, visit **Settings -> Bluetooth.** (More information about Bluetooth later in this guide)
	Airdrop	Tap on this symbol to control **Airdrop**. A blue circle means Airdrop is on; not blue means Airdrop is off. Tap and hold to see the Airdrop options.
		But what is Airdrop? Airdrop is a feature that allows sharing of content from your iPad and iPhone with other nearby 'Airdrop-enabled' Apple devices, using Bluetooth. No internet connection is required for Airdrop to work (although both Wi-Fi and Bluetooth must be turned ON.)

Exploring Control Centre

You choose who is allowed to Airdrop to you as below:

- **Receiving off** – No-one, Airdrop not enabled.

- **Contacts Only** – Only those who are in your **iCloud** Contacts, and are also using iCloud.

- **Everyone for 10 Minutes** – Anyone who is in range of your device. Reverts to Contacts Only after 10 minutes.

New Airdrop Everyone limitation of 10 minutes:
This is is a new security feature of in iOS/iPadOS 16.

Airdrop is available as an option in the 'Share' menu.

 Personal Hotspot

Turn **Personal Hotspot** on or off – Green circle means 'on', not green means 'off'.

Personal Hotspot allows your iPhone or cellular iPad to 'lend' its mobile data/internet to another device. Essentially, it turns the current device into a wireless modem that will appear in the Wi-Fi network list on nearby devices.

Nearby devices can join the Personal Hotspot if they are provided the password to this Personal Hotspot network.

Visit **Settings -> Personal Hotspot** to see and, if desired, reset the Personal Hotspot password.

 Media Controls

This section of Control Centre shows **what media is currently playing** (or paused) and allows you to start or pause playing (or skip back or forward). Tap and hold on this area to see further options – to scan through a track and control the volume.

- Press ▶ to play your music (or whatever other media is showing)

- Pause by pressing ❙❙

- Skip back and forward through tracks using ▶▶ and ◀◀

- Use the slider to move back and forward through the current track (move the dot back and forward). Use the volume slider at the bottom to adjust volume.

Exploring Control Centre

- Choose to send your music to another device – tap (the symbol at top right of the Media Controls window) and tap the applicable device from the list.
- If your device is not locked, you can also access the currently playing media app by tapping the track title.

 Rotation Lock **Rotation Lock** stops the screen from rotating when you turn it on its side or upside down. A white background with red symbol shows Rotation Lock is on; a grey background shows it is off.

 Mute Mute the device to stop noises from notifications and alerts. You can still play media while Mute is on. Red means Mute is On, white means Mute is Off. (Note. On the iPhone, the Mute function is enabled/disabled using the left-side top switch.)

 Focus allows you to set **Do Not Disturb** on temporarily, to stop and noises and notifications. It also allows you to turn on or off any of the other **Focus** types, where each of the Focus types allows you to allow or disallow certain notifications/apps at different times.

See more about the Do Not Disturb and Focus later in this guide.

 Brightness Control Slide the bar up and down to **adjust the brightness** of your screen.

Touch and hold to see some further options – for turning **Night Shift** on or off

Night Shift is a feature that gives your screen a different, warmer 'hue' at night. This is aimed at helping reduce sleep problems due to the 'blue light' usually emitted by the screen.

You can set your Night Shift to turn on and off on a schedule from **Settings -> Display and Brightness.**

 Volume Control Slide the bar up and down to **adjust the sound volume**. Slide down to the bottom to mute the volume

Exploring Control Centre

Screen Mirroring

Screen Mirroring is a feature that allows you to show (i.e. 'mirror') your iPad or iPhone screen on an **AirPlay** device.

This would normally be your Apple TV, which is a small device that you connect to your television via a HDMI cable. Under the latest Mac operating system, mobile Apple devices can now also be mirrored to a Mac computer.

Tap on **Airplay Mirroring** then tap on the applicable Airplay device to send your iPad/iPhone screen contents to that display.

Go to the same option (which will show the device that you are mirroring to) and tap '**Stop Mirroring**' when you no longer wish to send you display to the that other device.

Torch

Tap to turn the Torch on. This Control is only available on iPhones and iPad Pros with a flash.

Touch and hold on the torch symbol to control the brightness of the torch. Slide up to increase brightness, down to decrease.

Timer

Tap to access to Timer feature of the Clock app.

Or touch and hold to see a slider that allows you to quickly set a timer for the timeframe required.

Select **Start** to start the timer; Return here to stop it before the time is up.

Calculator

On iPhone only – gives quick access to the Calculator app. Touch and hold to have the option to 'Copy Last Result'. Turn the iPhone on its side to see more complex calculator functions.

Camera

The camera symbol gives quick access to the Camera App. Touch and hold to gain quick access to options to take a selfie, record a video, record slo-mo, or (on certain iPhones) take a portrait photo.

Exploring Control Centre

Add more controls to your Control Centre

Apple provides the capability to include additional controls and to customise your Control Centre.

This is done from **Settings -> Control Centre**.

A list of controls is shown, under the heading INCLUDED CONTROLS. These are the ones currently showing in your Control Centre.

Tap ⊖ to remove any control you don't want to see in Control Centre – and confirm by tapping **Remove**.

The bottom section, headed MORE CONTROLS, shows other controls that can optionally be included in Control Centre.

Tap ⊕ to add a control to the top section, and thereby include it in the Control Centre.

In the top section (the INCLUDED CONTROLS section), drag the ☰ symbol up and down to re-order the included controls in the Control Centre.

Limiting access to Control Centre

It is possible to control the places from which Control Centre is accessible.

While it is handy to be able to access the Control Centre from the Lock Screen, consider disabling this if you are security conscious.

This is done from the Settings app - **Settings -> Touch ID and Passcode** or **Settings -> Face ID & Passcode** (or Settings -> Passcode on older devices).

Set the **Control Centre** slider to off (not green) to prevent Control Centre access from the Lock Screen.

To avoid accidental displaying of Control Centre, some apps that rely on similar gestures (e.g. swiping up from near the bottom of the screen), such as maps and Camera, may require you to swipe up twice: once to reveal a

Exploring Control Centre

'handle' (a little bar at the bottom of the screen) for Control Centre and a second time to reveal Control Centre.

Alternatively, if you find it annoying that Control Centre pops up unnecessarily, you can just turn off the ability to access the Control Centre while you are using Apps.

Set the **Access Within Apps** setting to off (not green) in **Settings -> Control Centre.**

Managing your Home Screen Apps

Edit mode for your Home Screen

Have you ever wondered why your Apps have started wiggling, with many showing a little minus sign at the top left?

This happens when hold you your finger on a vacant area of the Home Screen for couple of seconds or so.

You have put your iPad or iPhone into **'App Edit'** mode.

Or, you may have touched and held on an app and chosen the option to **Edit Home Screen** from the mini menu that appeared.

Here's what you can do while those Apps are wiggling!

Stop that Wiggle

Tap **Done**, which appears at the top right of the screen when you are in the 'wiggle' mode or

- swipe up from the bottom of the screen if you don't have a Home Button OR
- press the Home Button if you have one.

Rearrange your Apps

While in this mode, you can move Apps around. Just hold your finger on an app until it pulses slightly then, without lifting your finger, drag it to its new position.

Let go when it is in its new position.

Any App that is used often can be dragged down onto the **'Dock'** at the bottom (so that it is available on all Home Screens). You may

Managing your Home Screen Apps

have to drag another app out first, as only a few apps can fit on the Dock (4 for iPhone, 13 for a standard sized iPad, and 15 for the biggest iPad).

Move an app to a different Home Screen

If you want an App on a different home screen, drag it to the edge of the screen and hold it there until the screen switches to next/previous home screen. Let go when it is on the screen and in the position you require.

Alternatively, touch and hold on an app and move it slightly. Then, while still holding onto that app with the first hand, swipe between screens with the other hand - until until you find the screen you require.

Drag the app to the new position on that screen, then let go of it.

Delete (or Remove) Apps

Touch and hold on the app you wish to delete, and you will see a menu with the **Remove App** option.

You will see a confirmation screen – tap **Delete App** to confirm the deletion from your device.

If you want to just remove the app from this Home Screen – and move it to a special area called the App Library (covered next) – choose **Remove from Home Screen.**

Alternatively, get your apps into 'wiggle mode' by touching and holding on any app for a couple of seconds – or by

Managing your Home Screen Apps

choosing **Edit Home Screen** in the menu that pops up when you first hold on the app.

To delete any app, tap on the ⊖ at the top left.

You will then see the same options as described above to 'delete' or 'remove' the app.

Any app that you delete is still recorded against your Apple ID as a 'purchased' App and can be re-downloaded any time without further cost.

If you have finished deleting, stop the wiggle using one of the methods described above.

An alternative way of deleting (or perhaps 'offloading' apps is to visit **Settings -> General -> iPhone Storage** (or **iPad Storage**). More on this later in this guide.

Group your Apps

If you have a lot of apps and lots of Home Screens, it can be hard to find the one you want.

Apple has provided a way to 'group' apps that are similar – this can reduce the number of Home Screens and sometimes make it easier to locate the app you are looking for.

As an example, if you have several games on your device for your kids or grandkids, you could pop all of these apps into a Games group so that they are out of your way!

As with deleting and rearranging apps, get the apps a-wiggling by holding your finger on any app for a second or two and choosing **Edit Home Screen**, or by touching and holding a vacant spot on the Home Screen.

Managing your Home Screen Apps

To group one app with another,

- Touch and hold the app that is to go into the group.

- Without lifting your finger, drag that app **ON TOP** of another app that you wish to put in the same group.

- An 'App group' will form with those two Apps in it.

- Take your finger off the screen to complete creation of the new group.

The new group will show a name that has been automatically allocated to it, based on the type of apps that you have put into it. Tap on the name to change it to a name of your own choice. Just press the ⓧ on the right of the group's name to delete and change it.

Adding/Removing Apps for an existing App Group

While the apps are still wiggling, you can add more Apps to the app group.

- Touch and hold on the App and drag it on top of the existing app group.

- Let go once it is on top of the group, and it should be added into that group.

- If you 'hover' the app over the group, the group will open up and you will be able to drag the app into a larger view of the group.

- Touch outside the app group to see the Home Screen again.

- Add further apps to the group as required.

Managing your Home Screen Apps

If you add enough apps that the group appears full (16 on iPad, 9 on iPhone) a second page will be created for that group when you add another app.

In the example below right, I dragged 17 apps from my iPad's first Home Screen into a group.

The 17th app that I dragged into the group is on the second screen in the app group. I must open the app group, then swipe from right to left to see the second screen for the group.

Just remember that you can only add apps to an app group – one app group cannot be added to another.

To remove an app from an App Group, just drag it to a spot that is outside the app group and hold it there until the App Group minimises, then drag the app to its new Home Screen position and let go.

HANDY HINT: Moving multiple apps in one go

You may find that you have the need to move more than one app at once. In the example above, I wanted to 'undo' the App Group that I created - but dragging that many apps out of the group one-by-one was going to be very tedious.

To move multiple apps in one hit, follow these steps:

- With your apps in Wiggle mode, put your finger on one of the apps and move it a little.

- While still holding that app, tap on the other apps you wish to move with your other hand.

- You will see each of the other tapped apps jump on top the already selected apps, and a number appear at top right of this stack of apps – showing how many apps are selected in the stack of apps

- Keep your finger on this stack of apps, and drag them to the new position, on the Home Screen or in an App Group.

- When you let go, the group will separate and show again as individual apps.

The App Library

iOS 14 brought a new feature to the iPhone – the App Library. This feature was then also made available for the iPad in iPadOS 15.

The App Library is found by swiping to the final Home Screen, then swiping right to left one more time.

The App Library reflects all the apps that are on your device, and groups them into categories for you.

The idea of it is that you can decide what key apps you want to see on your Home Screens, then let the rest reside in the App Library.

A very handy feature of the App Library is the ability to see all your App sorted into alphabetic order.

Simple tap the Search field at the top to see this alphabetic list (see image bottom right).

Any app that you see in this list, or in the categorised list (as shown top right) can be added to a Home Screen.

Simply touch and hold on the app to see some options.

Choose **Add to Home Screen** to put that App on a Home Screen. It will appear in the next available space on the second or subsequent screen.

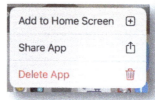

Alternatively, touch and hold on the App in the App Library then move it slightly – in which case the last Home Screen will appear, and you can use the same method as described earlier to move the app to the required Home Screen.

For new apps that you add to your device, you can choose whether they go onto the next available Home Screen, or whether they just get added to the App library and not to the Home Screen,

These options can be found in **Settings -> Home Screen** on the iPhone, or **Settings -> Home Screen & Multitasking** on the iPad.

Discovering Today View & Widgets!

What is Today view?

The Today view provides all sorts of information about today, news, weather, events, battery levels and much more.

The information shown is from 'widgets' that are provided by the apps on your device.

What are Widgets?

Widgets are big icons for apps that show some information from that app.

You get to customise what apps show their widget in the Today view AND on your Home Screens.

Viewing Today View

There are a few ways to get to the Today view.

- When you are viewing the Notification Centre, swipe left to right.

- Otherwise, swipe left to right when you are on the first Home Screen to reveal the Today view.

Editing the widgets that appear on your Home Screen and in the Today view is achieved by getting your apps into the 'Wiggle' mode (as covered in the previous section).

Look for the +

One thing that you may not have noticed before while in the 'wiggle' mode is that a + symbol appears at the top left of the screen – both on the Home Screens, and in the Today View

This + allows you to choose what widgets appear on that Home Screen or in the Today view.

Let's look first at the Today view, then we'll talk about the Widgets on the Home Screens.

Discovering Today View & Widgets!

Customising Today View

The first time you view the Today view, you should see a set of 'default' widgets in this view.

To get the Today view into 'Edit'/'Wiggle' mode, hold your finger on any widget and choose **Edit Home Screen**.

Alternatively, hold your finger on a vacant area of the screen to invoke the 'wiggle'. Or scroll to the bottom of the list of Today widgets and tap **Edit**.

You can also get Today view into Edit/Wiggle mode from the Home Screen, then swipe from left to right to uncover the wiggling Today view – ready for editing.

While in this Edit/Wiggle mode, tap an any widget to amend its settings (if any are available) or drag the widgets up and down to change the order.

Tap ⊖ symbol on top left of a widget to remove that widget.

While the widgets wiggle, you will see the + symbol at top left, which will allow you to add new widgets.

Tap + to first view some suggested widgets to add to Today.

On the iPad, the + option provides a sidebar that shows the 'Suggestions' option, then the set of apps that have available widgets.

On the iPhone, scroll down past the 'Suggestions' to see all the apps that offer widgets.

Tap on any app in the list to then see the options for the size of the widget.

Discovering Today View & Widgets!

The 'dots' towards the bottom show how many options exist (see image on right).

Swipe right to left to see the other sizes. Choose **Add Widget** when you find the size you want for your widget.

Your Widget will then be added to the Today view as the last widget in the list.

While still in 'edit'/'wiggle' mode, you can then drag that widget up or down in the list, to set its position.

If you decide you don't want to add the widget that you tapped,

- on iPhone tap the x at top right.
- on the iPad, tap the area above the window that popped up OR press the Home Button (if you have one) or swipe up from the bottom (if you don't have a Home Button).

Discovering Smart Stacks

There is also the option to add a **Smart Stack.**

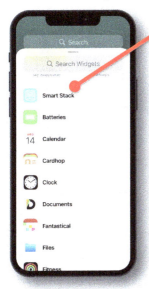

Discovering Today View & Widgets!

A Smart Stack is a widget that contains multiple other widgets, and that you can scroll/rotate through.

Once again, you choose the size of the Smart Stack widget by swiping through the available size options, then choosing **Add Widget**.

This will add the stack widget in the last position. Drag it up or down, to the position where it should sit in the list of widgets.

To customise the content of the stack, tap on the stack widget while it is still wiggling.

Tap the 'minus' sign at top left to remove any app that you don't want to see in the stack. Touch and hold, then drag the app up/down to reposition it in the list of stack apps. To exit editing of the stack widget, tap **Done** at top right.

While the widgets are wiggling, you can drag other widgets *of the same size* on top of that stack to add the widget to that stack.

You can also start a new stack by dragging a widget on top of another widget of the same size.

If the **Smart Rotate** option at the top is 'On' (circle is blue) then your Smart Stack will automatically reflect the widget that your device deems most applicable/appropriate based on your use of the device.

There are other more basic widgets

You can find even more widgets – widgets that can only appear in the Today view and not on a Home Screen.

While the wiggle is still active, go to the bottom of the list of widgets and choose the **Customise** option.

This will show some more basic app widgets that can't be used in stacks and don't give you different size options.

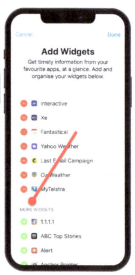

Discovering Today View & Widgets!

Scroll through to the **MORE WIDGETS** list in the second section (see last image on previous page).

Tap the green '+' to add app widgets to the top section.

In the top section, tap the red '-' to remove widgets.

Drag the 'triple-line' symbol up and down to re-arrange the order.

Select **Done** at top right to finish.

You will notice when your Apps are wiggling that these apps are in a separate section towards the bottom of the Today view, with a 'grey' background.

In the example on the right, the widgets from that titled 'Interactive' onwards do not show a symbol at top left – so are these more basic widgets.

If you want to remove any of these widgets, choose the **Customise** option again when you are in wiggle mode, and choose ⊖ to remove that widget.

To exit Today View

Simply swipe right to get out of Today view and return to your first Home screen. Tap Done at top right if you have completed your edits.

Widgets on your Home Screen

While we have focused above on the Today view and the widgets that appear there, you can ALSO add widgets to ANY of your Home Screens.

And these widgets can be made into Stacks if they are the same size.

You may find that you prefer to view your widgets in this way, instead of (or perhaps in addition to) using the Today view.

As mentioned earlier, you will notice that, when the apps are in their 'wiggle' mode, there is the same + symbol at top left (same as what we see in the Today view).

The same then applies as for the Today view – add multiple widgets if you like, and stack them up if they are the same size.

Once they are added to your Home Screen, you can drag them around to the position required – just like you can with Apps that are wiggling. And you can move Widgets between Home Screens – just like you can do with Apps.

Multi-Tasking & App Switching

Multi-tasking is a feature of the iPhone and iPad that allows you to easily and quickly switch between different apps that you are using.

When you switch back to an app you were using, you can pick up right where you left off.

Switch between apps

Follow these steps to switch quickly between apps:

1. On both the iPad and iPhone with a Home Button: **Double-click the Home button**
2. On the iPad and on an iPhone without a Home Button: **Drag up** from below the bottom of the screen **to the middle of the screen** and stop
3. This will show the Multi-tasking screen (also known as the App Switching screen).

4. **Swipe left or right** and locate the app you want use.
5. **Tap the required app** to switch to it.

Handy Hint: Drag to switch between Apps

A quick way is to drag from left to right at the bottom of the screen to go to the previous app, or right to left to go back the other way.

Multi-tasking & App Switching (and how to fix a misbehaving App)

Squashing that myth about frequent closing of apps

For those of you who have been told that it is necessary to regularly come to this multi-tasking screen to 'close' your apps – supposedly to avoid wasting battery and/or data - THIS IS NOT TRUE!

In fact, the regular 'closing of apps can actually cause the opposite effect to that intended.

I usually only bother to 'swipe up' an app if I am having a problem – otherwise, I rarely bother to do this.

Viewing two apps at once (iPad only)

Later model iPads have several further multi-tasking options. The availability of these features will depend on the model of iPad that you are using.

With iPadOS 15, the way you managed viewing of more than one app at once – for the better! Let's first look at the options available.

Slide Over

The **Slide Over** feature on the iPad allows you to open a second app without closing the one you are in, showing the current app in a smaller 'floating' window over the top of the bigger window.

In the example on the right, the Photos app is a 'Slide Over', with the Mail app in full screen.

As an example of where this is useful, I can now drag and drop a photo from the Photos app into a Mail message.

Split View

The **Split View** feature allows you to view two apps at once, so that you can work with them both concurrently.

In Split View, the split can be 50/50 to 25/75, or 75/25.

Viewing two apps at once

Changes to Split Screen and Slide Over since iPadOS 15

Since iPadOS 15, there is now a set of 3 dots at the top of every app screen that supports Split Screen or Slide Over.

Tapping these dots provides a set of 4 options.

Tapping the **Full Screen** option will take the app into 'full screen' mode if it wasn't in that mode already.

Split View allows you to select a second app to show on the screen at the same time as the current app.

If **Split View** is chosen, the current app's window will disappear off to the left side, allowing for the selection of the second app – which will then appear on the right side of the screen.

The **Slide Over** option will make the <u>current</u> app the 'Slide Over' app. If your screen was already in Split View, other app will become full screen.

If only the current app was showing when Slide Over was chosen, the current app will disappear off to the right side of the screen, so that you can then tap to choose the app that will appear as the main full screen app, underneath the Slide Over app.

If an app does not show the ... symbol at the top, then it means that the app cannot be part of a Split Screen and cannot be used in Slide Over mode.

Tapping Close will close the app.

Viewing two apps at once

Alternative Method of activating Slide Over

Here are the steps to open an App in Slide Over mode, as applied in iPadOS 14 (and are still available in iPadOS 16). Note that, in the below images and description, the line at the top of Slide Over screen has been replaced with the ... symbol in iPadOS 16.

1. **Drag up** (not too far) from the bottom of the screen to show the Dock (see image on right). It will sit on top of your active app.

2. **Touch and hold, then start dragging** the required app from the Dock. In the example on the right, it is the Photos app that is being dragged into Slide Over mode.

3. **Let go of the app** and it will appear on top of the active previous app, over to the right (see image on right). You can then interact with that 'mini' version of the app in the same way that you normally would.

For the example I am showing in the fourth image on right that I can drag a photo from the Powder Room album onto the Note that I am creating, to show photos from a renovation.

I can then look for another photo from the Photos Slide Over and drag that across onto my Note.

Add more Slide Over Apps

You can have multiple apps available in the Slide Over window.

To see all the apps that I have open in Slide Over mode, simply drag the bar at the bottom of the Slide Over screen upwards slightly. This then gives an 'app switcher' for all active Slide Over apps, allowing the choice (by tapping) of which

Viewing two apps at once

one should be the active (front) app for Slide Over. Any app no longer required in Slide Over mode can be swiped upwards to remove it from the list.

I can also drag the bar at the bottom of the Slide Over window screen from left to right and right to left to move between the apps that are available in Slide Over mode.

Moving & Removing the Slide Over Screen

The Slide Over screen can then be moved from side-to-side.

Position your finger on the dots (previously a line in iPadOS 14) at top middle of the Slide Over screen and drag to move it.

If you want the Slide Over screen out of the way for a while, just touch this symbol and drag it off the screen, to the right or left.

Alternatively, swipe up the line that appears at the bottom of the Slide Over screen to temporarily get rid of the Slide Over

An arrow will appear briefly on the left or right edge, to indicate that there is a Slide Over screen available.

You can then bring it back by sliding it back onto the screen from outside the right or left side of the screen (depending on where it went originally).

Alternative method of activating Split View

The old method of activating **Spit View** is still available in iPadOS 16 and is similar to activating **Slide Over** mode under iPadOS 14.

Instead of 'dropping' the chosen second app onto somewhere in the middle of the screen, drag it to the very far right or left of the screen so that the screen 'splits' (as shown in the third image below), then let go (see fourth image – next page).

Viewing two apps at once

Adjusting the Split

There will be a little verticle **App Divider Bar** between the apps that show in Split View.

Give both apps equal space: Drag the App Divider Bar to the middle of the screen.

Give one app more space than the other: Drag the App Divider Bar to the required position.

To Close Split View: Drag the App Divider Bar all the way to the left or right, depending on which app you wish to close.

To change from Slide Over to Split Screen view

Touch on the ... symbol at top of the Slide Over screen (previously a bar) and drag it towards the far right or far left, until it pops into Split screen view.

Or simply tap on the ... and choose **Split View**, then choose **Left Split** or **Right Split**.

To change from Split Screen to Slide Over view

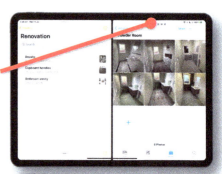

Tap ... at top of the App that needs to be the Slide Over app and choose **Slide Over**. Or touch on the ... symbol at top (previously a bar) and drag it downwards onto the other app screen to put it into Slide Over view.

Combine Split Screen and Slide Over

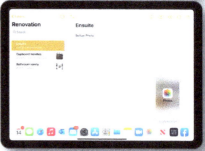

You can add a Slide Over screen to your Split Screen – effectively allowing you to see 3 apps at once.

Viewing two apps at once

Split Screen and Slide Over can be the same app

You can use these multi-screen features to see two 'windows' of the same app at once – which can help when referencing or organizing within that app.

The Close option

If you wish to close an app that is one of the Split Screen or Slide Over apps, tap ... at top and choose **Close**.

Picture in Picture

The **Picture in Picture** feature allows you to work in other apps as you're watching a movie or using FaceTime.

When watching a video, TV program or video Podcast, or perhaps in a Zoom meeting or Facetime call, press the Home Button/swipe up (depending on your device) or tap the picture-in-picture icon that may be visible in some cases (e.g at top left in Apple TV app).

You will then see the video window reduce in size and position itself (usually) at the top right of the screen, with control symbols at the bottom for controlling the video/app (as shown in the image below).

1. **Resize the video window**: Pinch open or closed to make the video window larger or smaller.

Viewing two apps at once

2. **Move the video window**: Drag the window to move it out of the way or into a new position.

3. **Return video to full screen**: Tap the picture-in-picture icon again to resume watching in full screen mode.

4. **To close Picture in Picture**: Press ✗

Finding things - Spotlight Search

What is Spotlight Search?

The Spotlight Search feature of your iPad and iPhone allows you to search for anything that is on your device.

For example, this could be an App that you can't locate, but that you know is somewhere on a Home Screen.

Perhaps you want to find all the Messages and Mail that you have sent to and received from a particular person.

Perhaps you want to quickly locate the Contact card for someone whose address you need.

By just typing just a few letters, you will see a list of everything that matches the search phrase you have typed. It's that easy! No need to find the relevant app first to get to that information!

You'll find more and more reasons to use Spotlight Search once you have discovered it!

But where is this great feature to be found?

To open Spotlight Search, just touch somewhere <u>in the middle of</u> the screen (**not at the top of the screen**), and then drag your finger downwards. Or, on certain iPhones, you can now tap the 'Search' option above the Dock (which changes to 'dots' when you start swiping right to left and left to right to see your various Home Screens).

Finding things - Spotlight Search

Three things will appear:

1. A **Search** bar will appear – at the top on the iPad, and just above the keyboard on the iPhone. (Note. The position of the iPhone's search bar changed in iOS 16 – it used to be at the top.)

2. **SIRI SUGGESTIONS** will show some suggested apps – the apps shown here will be determine based on your typical App usage.

3. You may also see some previous searches that you have performed – in case you need them again.

4. The on-screen keyboard will appear at the bottom (assuming you don't have a separate physical keyboard in use, in which case no keyboard appears).

Note. Siri Suggestions and recent searches can be turned off if you don't want to see them. Visit **Settings -> Siri & Search**, and turn off **Show Suggestions** and **Show Recents**.

Spotlight Search changes in iOS 16

As mentioned above, the Spotlight Search search bar has moved to just above the keyboard on the iPhone in iOS 16 – while staying at the top of the screen on the iPad.

You will also notice on some iPhones (those without a Home Button) that you now have a Search option at the bottom of the Home Screen.

Finding things - Spotlight Search

Searching using Spotlight Search

To search using this function, just start typing the name of the 'thing' that you are looking for!

If you lose your keyboard, touch on the **Search** field at the top again to make the keyboard re-appear. (Again, this is assuming that you don't have a separate physical keyboard.)

For example, I am going to look for my Weather App, which is on one of the several Home Screens on my iPad.

It might even be hidden away in an 'App Group', making it quite difficult to find.

As I start typing letters in the Search field at the top, a list of matches appears in a list below the Search field. Even after I just type the 'W', a list of Apps (and other things) starting with the letter 'W' will appear.

To select one of the items from the list of apps, just touch on it to be taken straight to that item. For example, touching **Oz Weather** in the above list will open that App.

If there are mail messages listed, touching on one of the **mail messages** will open the **Mail** app at that specific mail message.

If there are **Contacts** showing in the list of matching items, touching on a **Contact** would open the **Contacts** app, with that person's details on display.

On the iPad, to make the keyboard disappear temporarily so that you can see the full list that is hidden behind the keyboard, on the iPad you must touch the bottom right-hand key on the keyboard. Or just press the '**go**' key on the keyboard.

Finding things - Spotlight Search

On both the iPad and the iPhone, scrolling through the results also causes the keyboard to disappear. Tap the Search bar to bring it back.

You can see that this can give you a very quick way of getting to information and Apps that are on your iPad or iPhone.

Finding 'lost' apps!

I use Spotlight Search most for quickly accessing Apps that are not on the first Home Screen or that are hidden away in App Groups.

A very helpful feature of Spotlight Search is that for Apps, the 'App Group' in which the App resides (if it is in a group) will be shown alongside the App's name, on the right-hand side.

In the example of **podcasts** above, the App can be found in an App Group by the name of Apple.

If you are desperately trying find a particular App that is hidden away, this may help you in your search!

Search the Web using Spotlight Search?

Here's one of the great uses for Spotlight Search that many people would not even consider!

If you need to search for something on the internet, why not just go to your Spotlight Search and enter your search phrase there? As an example, I have entered Dinosaur in the search field here. I know that I don't have anything with Dinosaur on my iPad – but look at the options that I get when I type in something like this!

Finding things - Spotlight Search

In the example above, by choosing the result that has the Safari symbol, Spotlight search takes me straight to Safari and does a Google Search for the search phrase that I entered in Spotlight Search!

This saves me from having to find the Safari app on my Home Screen, tap on it, then tap on the Search field in Safari, then enter my search phrase there.

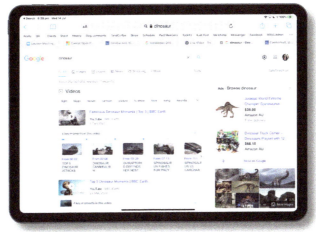

Try this method of searching for a web page next time! Maybe you just want to look up the phone number of a restaurant – enter its name (and perhaps its suburb) in Spotlight Search.

But why is Spotlight Search showing me something I don't need?

If you bring up your Spotlight Search but find that there are already some details showing on your screen, this will be the 'last search' that you did with Spotlight Search.

For example, if I go to Spotlight Search again when I last typed 'weather', I need to clear out my previous search phrase so I can do a new search.

Touch on the Ⓧ on the right-hand side of the Search bar to remove the previous search phrase. This will clear the screen of results and allow for the entry of a new search phrase.

Alternatively, use the backspace key to remove the previous search phrase.

Finding things - Spotlight Search

Do calculations and conversions

You can even type in a calculation in the Search Bar – the result will show as you progressively type your equation.

Typing something like '30 Celsius in Fahrenheit' will quickly give the result.

Get weather details

Typing something like 'weather in Sydney' gives the current temperature in the place you chose, plus forecast information. Tap on the weather information provided to jump straight to the weather app and details of the weather for that place.

And more

Calculate exchange rates (type "A$100 in USD"), get movie session times (just type "movies" and scroll down to see the list of available movies), play a song (type "play songbird"), check flight progress (by typing in a flight number) – just to name a few.

Volume Control & Muting

You can use the buttons on side of the iPad and iPhone to adjust the audio volume for music, movies, ringtones, etc.

On an iPad in 'portrait' orientation, volume controls are on the right side, towards the top. Or, if the iPad is in 'landscape' orientation, the volume controls are at top left)

On the iPhone, volume controls are at left side, towards the top.

The **TOP** button turns your **VOLUME UP.**

The **BOTTOM** button lower turns the **VOLUME DOWN**.

This assumes that you are holding your iPad/iPhone in portrait mode.

If you hold down the VOLUME DOWN button for an extended period, this will mute the device.

On the iPhone, the small switch above the volume controls is a 'mute' switch. This switch allows you to mute a ringing phone and stop other sounds and audio.

When the red bar is showing (as in this image), your device is muted (so will make no sound when it rings).

Flick it to the right to un-mute your iPhone.

Customising Sounds

You've probably noticed that your iPad or iPhone makes certain sounds to indicate different types of notifications, alerts and events - for example, the 'whoosh' sound of an email being sent, the noise it makes when an email or text arrives, the 'ringtone' of phone calls.

You get to choose the sounds that your iPad/iPhone makes when certain 'events' occur. Go to the **Settings -> Sounds and Haptics** (just **Settings -> Sounds** on iPad)

Choose your Ringer Volume

You also have the option for defining how loud the **Ringer and Alert Volume** should be, and whether the volume buttons should be able to change this (see image above).

If you have been finding that your ringer is not loud enough when your phone rings, it could be that your **Ringer and Alerts Volume** is turned down. Drag the dot to the required level to adjust.

If you don't want the ringer volume to be changed by the Volume buttons of your device, leave the **Change with Buttons** option off (not green).

Choose your Sounds

Below that you will see a list of **SOUND AND HAPTIC PATTERNS** (or just Sounds on the iPad). This is where you can customise the sounds that will apply for the key types of 'events' on your device.

For each event, the list will show (on the right) the name of the sound that currently applies to each of the events. On right is the screen that appears if I tap **Ringtone**.

The sound that is currently selected will be ticked. To listen to this sound, tap on its name. To change the sound,

Customising Sounds

tap on another sound name – and you will hear what it sounds like. Leave it ticked if you like it; otherwise, choose a different sound.

You will note that the list of sounds has two sections – one headed RINGTONES and the other headed ALERT TONES.

Ringtones are longer sounds; Alert Tones are shorter, sharper sounds. Have a play! It's quite fun going through all the sounds and finding one that suits your personality.

And, if you don't find the sound you like, you can always go to the **Tone Store** and purchase one!

Haptic Settings

Scroll to the end of the **Sounds and Haptics** options for some further options.

These options allow you to control whether you feel or hear **Keyboard Feedback** when you are typing (option is Keyboard Clicks on iPad), and whether your device makes the **Lock Sound** when it is put to sleep, or the cover is closed.

The final options relate to the 'vibrate/tap' sensation you get when you do certain things – such as touching and holding on an app on the Home Screen. These are known as Haptics.

You will feel a gentle tap when you do this. But this can be turned off using the **System Haptics** switch shown here.

There are also some new options above that to control the Haptics when in Ring or Silent mode.

Headphone Safety

Scrolling back to the top of the **Sounds and Haptics** options, you will see that there is now also a section titled **HEADPHONE AUDIO**.

On the iPhone, this contains the **Headphone Safety** option. Tap to see settings that allow you to receive a notification if the audio level is too high, and to set your device to **Reduce Loud Sounds** to protect your hearing.

On the iPad, there is just the **Reduce Loud Sounds** option available, allowing the setting of a maximum acceptable decibel level.

89

Understanding and Controlling Notifications

What is a Notification?

A Notification is a message that appears on your iPad or iPhone, advising that something has happened on the device.

For example, you have received a message, a call has arrived, something has updated, a News item has arrived, it is your turn in a game, and more.

It may be an alert reminding you about an appointment in your calendar, or a task that you have entered as a Reminder.

Define general and app-level Notification settings

In **Settings -> Notifications**, you define the Notification Styles for each of the apps on your device that produces alerts of some sort. (Not all apps do this.)

The list of apps is shown in the bottom part of the screen, under the NOTIFICATION STYLE heading.

As an example, the third screen below shows the Notification Style screen I get when I tap the Messages app in the list of apps.

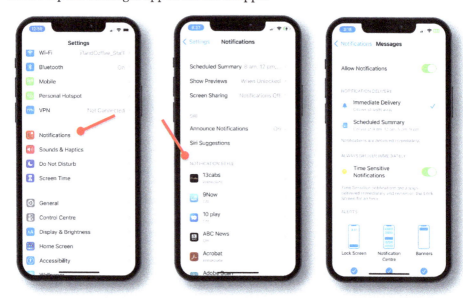

We'll shortly look at the Notification Style settings for each app. But let's first look at some other options that appear in the main Notifications screen (above centre).

Understanding and Controlling Notifications

Settings applicable to all Notifications

There are a few options that apply to all Notifications, found in **Settings -> Notifications**.

New Display As option for Notifications

New in iOS 16 (iPhone only) is the **DISPLAY AS** option, which allows you choose how you wish your Notifications

Below is Apple's description of these options – although I have struggled to see the difference between the settings when I have tried each of them out. (Maybe due to a current 'glitch' with the operating system.)

- Count: Displays the total number of notifications at the bottom of the screen. You can tap the count to see notifications.
- Stack: Displays notifications stacked at the bottom of the screen, with the most recent notification at the top.
- List: Displays notifications in a list.

Scheduled Summary

With iOS/iPadOS 15, Apple provided a new option for scheduling notifications – allowing you to defer app notifications until a nominated set of scheduled times.

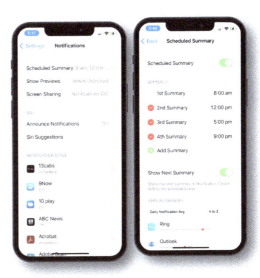

For each app then, you can choose whether its notifications are 'scheduled' or 'immediate'.

Tap the **Scheduled Summary** option to see the set of options available.

Add Summary allows you to nominate a time for a particular summary to be published.

As shown in the rightmost image here, I have set up several times for my summaries.

Scrolling down, I can then see the list of 'notifying' apps on my device.

Understanding and Controlling Notifications

I can view these apps in order of the most frequent notification averages or choose to view them in alphabetical order.

By turning the 'switch' for an app to the 'on' position (green), I can choose to defer any notifications from that app until the scheduled time – rather than seeing them immediately.

That same 'scheduled' setting for the app's notification can also be set when looking at the Notification Style for the app (covered shortly).

If I don't want to set such a schedule for notifications, I simply turn off **Scheduled Summary** – and this hides all the other options.

Show Previews

The next Notification setting is one that is important from a security perspective.

The **Show Previews** option controls what information about the notification is shown when the device is locked.

It is best to choose the **When Unlocked** option instead of **Always**.

You never know when you might get a confidential message that you don't want someone else to see.

This means that, if an alert appears when the screen is locked, the detail of any alert is not shown until the screen is unlocked – either with Face ID (or Touch ID, if applicable) or the Passcode.

On the right are examples of a Reminders alert that appears on the lock screen.

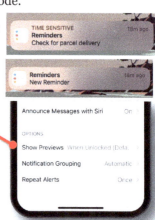

The top one is where **Show Previews** is set to **Always**, and the bottom one is where **Show Previews** is set to **When Unlocked**.

The option to **Show Previews** can also be set on an App by App basis. It is available at the bottom of the set of options for each App (which we will look at shortly).

Understanding and Controlling Notifications

Screen Sharing

The Screen Sharing option in Notifications was a new feature of iOS/iPadOS 15.

This setting allows you to disable notifications when you are using a new feature called **SharePlay** or using **Screen Mirroring** to show your device's screen on a bigger screen. This could be on a TV, or when you are on a Zoom.

As a rule, it is best to leave this setting switched 'off' (not green), as shown in the image above right.

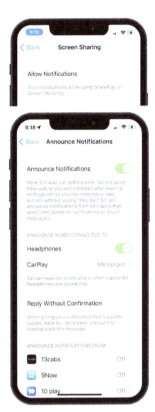

Announce Notifications

The **Announce Notifications** option allows you to choose to hear notifications 'out loud' when you are connected to headphones or Car Play.

When headphones are connected, notifications will be read out for each of the apps listed at the bottom with on 'On' setting.

Tap any app that is 'off' to enable these 'out loud' notifications.

For CarPlay, announced notifications only applies to Messages.

Notification Style per App

Each of the settings we have described above can also be adjusted on a 'per app basis', by tapping on the app's name in the main **Notifications** screen.

Allowing Notifications

This screen allows you to choose to completely turn off Notifications for the selected App – by turning the **Allow Notifications** switch to 'off' (not green).

Understanding and Controlling Notifications

If **Allow Notifications** is on, you will see the options for **Immediate Delivery** or **Scheduled Summary**, to choose the delivery mode for this particular app (which I could also set from the **Scheduled Summary** setting described earlier).

Time Sensitive Notifications

You can also choose to enable or disable **Time Sensitive Notifications** for the individual app. **Time Sensitive Notifications** are a feature of **Focus** (covered next), where you can choose to disable notifications for periods of times but still allow through notifications that are deemed 'time sensitive' (eg. reminders, calendar alerts, etc).

If the **Time Sensitive Notifications** setting has been enabled in **Focus**, you can then choose to turn off this feature for individual apps from within the Notification setting for the app.

Alert Types

If the **Allow Notifications** switch is on, you then choose where you see any Alerts generated by the app.

There are three options shown – **Lock Screen** (ie alerts are shown when the screen is locked), **Notification Centre** (which we will cover a bit further down) and **Banners** (which appear at the top of the screen when the device is in use).

Tick or untick to turn on or off that type of alert for the app. You can have all three turned on if desired.

On the left is an example of a Banner, showing a notification from the Reminders app.

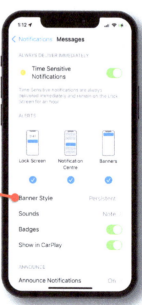

These Banners can be one of two styles (set via the **Banner Style** setting):

- **Persistent** – the Banner stays at the top of the screen until you do something to make it go away – by swiping up, or by tapping on the message to go to the app that generated the notification

- **Temporary** – the banner appears briefly at the top of the screen, then disappears.

Understanding and Controlling Notifications

Just some of the options available for the app's notifications/alerts are:

- **Badges** (right) – Show a red circled number on an app icon, thereby showing you that there is something waiting on your action or attention in that App.
- **Sounds** - a sound can play when the notification occurs. For some apps, you can customise the sound from the Notifications settings (as is the case for Messages in the example above right). For other apps, you can simply choose whether to play a sound or not.
- **Show in CarPlay** – if you have a car with CarPlay, you can choose whether alerts generated by the app appear there (only applicable to Messages)

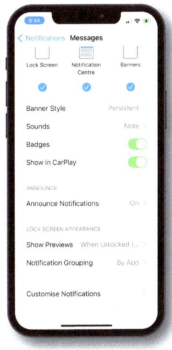

Announce Notifications

Define here whether 'out loud' Notifications should apply for this app when you are wearing Headphones.

Lock Screen Appearance

In the app-specific Notification settings, you can choose to change the default set at the 'all apps' level for both the **Show Previews** and **Notification Grouping** options.

For example, you may want to allow Previews on the Lock Screen for most apps, but just not for Messages and Mail apps. And you may want to Group notifications from certain apps but not others.

Customise Notifications

The **Customise Notifications** option is available for only Messages, allowing you to choose whether you want to repeat the alert if you have not yet read the message, and whether Notifications should appear if the sender is Unknown.

I choose to turn off notifications from Unknown Senders, as they are usually spam!

Understanding and Controlling Notifications

The Notification Centre

The **Notification Centre** is a feature of your iPad and iPhone that appears when you swipe downwards from **above the top middle or left of the screen**.

It also appears when you drag upwards slightly on the Lock Screen (as described earlier).

It shows the recent Notifications that have occurred – those whose apps are allowed to record their details in the Notification Centre.

Tap on any alert you see there to jump straight to the app and that item.

Or touch and hold on an alert to see further options (for some notifications only).

This touch and hold gesture is particularly handy for Reminder alerts – as it allows you to **Mark as Completed**, or request that the reminder come back again at a later time.

The notifications that show on the Lock Screen and in Notification Centre may be grouped by App, depending on your Notification settings for that app

In the example on the left there are multiple News story notifications (hard to see with the black background!).

Tapping on the notification shown expands the stack (see leftmost image on next page).

Understanding and Controlling Notifications

^ Show Less (only ^ on iPhone) will then summarise them again under the most recent notification (see previous image).

Manage Notifications from the Notification Centre

Swiping a notification (or group of notifications) from right to left will provide further options (as shown in middle image above, indicated by red line).

- **Clear** (or **Clear All** if you swipe a 'group' of notifications) will remove the notification/s from the Notification Centre (example indicated by red line above)
- **Options** (rightmost image above) gives some other options for quickly managing the Notifications generated by this app – either temporarily or more permanently.

  It includes the ability to quickly access the Settings for the app's Notifications.

And for those apps whose notifications you deem unnecessary, you can quickly **Turn Off** notifications from those apps.

Understanding and Controlling Notifications

Make your iPhone flash when there is a Notification

The LED light (which is the camera flash) at the back of your iPhone and iPad Pro can be used as a notifying beacon, so that you can see when alerts occur or calls come in!

This is great for cases where the sound is turned off, or for finding your ringing iPhone at the bottom of your handbag!

This feature can be turned on in an area of **Settings** called **Accessibility**.

(Accessibility in an area in Settings that has various options and settings to assist people who have vision, hearing, and motor impairments.)

Go to **Settings > Accessibility**.

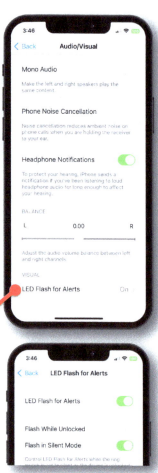

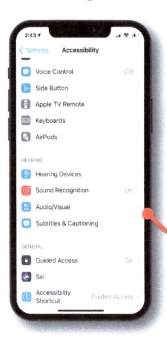

The options in the first two sections in Accessibility are designed to assist those with vision and motor impairment.

The third section of options has 'Hearing' settings. The setting we are looking for is actually one to assist those with hearing impairment.

Tap **Audio Visual**.

Tap **LED Flash for Alerts** to make your phone flash whenever a notification is received.

Turn on the first option, then choose whether the flash should occur while unlocked and whether it should occur in Silent mode.

Focus & Do Not Disturb

The Focus options

The iPad and iPhone have a set of options that allow you control what apps and services are allowed to distract and notify you at different times of day and on different days of the week. There are several options for controlling these things.

These controls are called Focus – extending the original Do Not Disturb functionality that applied prior to iOS 15 to five different categories instead: Do Not Disturb, Driving, Personal, Sleep and Work.

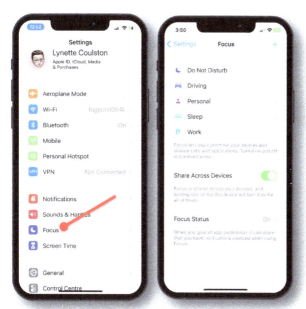

Each of the different types of Focus allow you to define what is allowed to 'get through' when the Focus type is active.

Depending on the Focus type, you can define which people get through (via phone, Messages, etc), notifications from which apps get through, what Home Screens you see, a schedule for the Focus type and more.

We won't go through all the different Focus types in this guide.

Various Focus Option changes

iOS/iPadOS 16 has brought several changes to the options provided under the Focus set of options. Hopefully these make this complex area easier to use. I must say though, that I only really use the Do Not Disturb feature, so will only cover that in this guide. Other Focus types work in a similar way and offer similar features.

One of the significant changes that you will notice for Do Not Disturb and other Focus types is that you can now have a customized Lock Screen and Home Screen associated with a Focus Type – so that it is obvious when that Focus is in operation.

We will cover the changes to Lock Screens a bit further on in this guide.

Focus & Do Not Disturb

Do Not Disturb

The **Do Not Disturb** settings of Focus allow you to set a schedule, defining when your device needs to be 'silent' and, when it is in this 'do not disturb' mode, whether there are any exceptions to this 'do not disturb' rule.

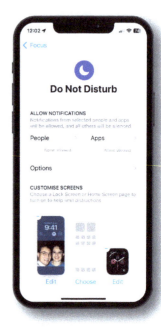

When the **Do Not Disturb** mode is active (i.e. slider shows green) and has its default settings, your device will not make a sound if there are any phone calls (in case of iPhone), messages, emails, Facetime calls or other alerts or notifications.

The exception to this is if you have set an Alarm, a timer or set off the **Emergency SOS** – these will override the **Do Not Disturb** mode.

With the new Focus settings, you can choose to customise which people and apps are exceptions to the 'do not disturb' rule.

Set a schedule for Do Not Disturb (similar for other Focus categories)

To set up a **Do Not Disturb** schedule, go to **Settings -> Focus -> Do Not Disturb**, and tap **Add Schedule**.

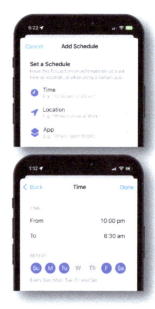

Focus & Do Not Disturb

To set the schedule for your **Do Not Disturb**, tap the **Add Schedule** option, then set the from and to time that should apply.

You can also choose to disable this setting for certain days of the week, by tapping any days that the settings shouldn't apply to (so they turn grey).

Then choose **Done** at top right to establish the setting for **Do Not Disturb** (or whichever Focus type you chose).

You will also see that the Focus schedule can be set based on a Location, or for when you are using a particular app. In the example above, I have set my Do Not Disturb to turn on whenever I am using Zoom.

Allow or Silence selected people for this Focus

Tap the **People** option, then choose if you want to

- **Silence Notifications From** for a nominated set of people (and allow others through), or to

- **Allow Notifications From** a specifically selected set of people.

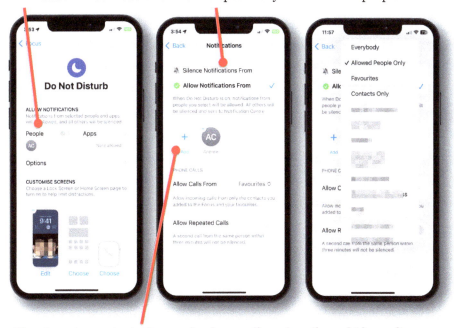

Then tap + to nominate the people who are allowed or silenced (depending on your choice at the top)

If you have chosen the **Allow Notifications From** option, you will see an **Allow Calls From** option under the **PHONE CALLS** section.

Focus & Do Not Disturb

Tap this to choose what calls should be allowed through when **Do Not Disturb** Focus type is active. You can set up a custom List of Contacts in the Contact app (new in iOS 16) and choose that list here. Or limit callers to Favourites, Contacts only, or just the people Added in the section above.

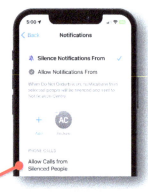

The **Repeated Calls** option on that screen (se middle screen above) allows you to choose to let through calls (phone OR Facetime) that seem urgent – where someone calls you twice within 3 minutes.

Be wary of leaving this on, as you can have your iPhone 'go off' at times when you really don't want this (e.g. church, movies, etc).

If you have chosen the Silence Notifications From option instead, the PHONE CALLS section only has the option to **Allow Calls from Silenced People**.

Allow certain apps to get through

If there are certain apps that you want to make exceptions to the **Do Not Disturb** (or other Focus type) rule, tap **Apps** under **Allowed Notifications**.

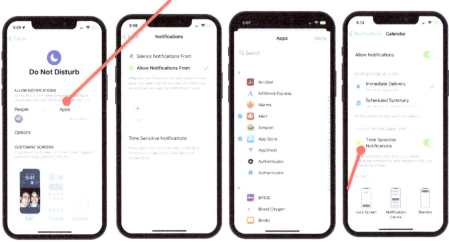

Once again, choose between Silencing or Allowing – same as applied for People.

Tap + and select (by tapping) the app or apps that should be silenced or allowed, then **Done** (top right) to finish.

Also available is the option to allow or disallow **Time Sensitive Notifications** from applicable apps. (This is a setting that can be enabled or disabled in Notifications, for certain Apple apps, like Messages, Calendar, Reminders and more – see example on right.)

Focus & Do Not Disturb

Manually set your 'Do Not Disturb'

While you would normally set up the **Do Not Disturb** (or other Focus) feature to operate according to its schedule (or perhaps your location), there may be times when it is important that your device temporarily operates under the '**Do Not Disturb**' rules.

For situations like these, you can manually switch on your **Do Not Disturb** (or any other Focus mode) from your device's **Control Centre**.

Simply tap the Focus option in the Control Centre, then tap the **Do Not Disturb** (or other Focus option) to turn it on (or off, if it is already on).

Even better, to turn on the feature of a shorter period, tap on the ... option to uncover some further options for setting limits on the **Do Not Disturb** period.

I prefer to set my **Do Not Disturb** using one of the options shown under the ... Otherwise, it is very easy to forget you have the **Do Not Disturb** (or other Focus) feature turned on, and miss important call, texts, etc.

New in iOS 16 (iPhones only)

The Focus types can now be linked to your custom Lock Screens, so that it is obvious from the lock and home screen background just which Focus is active. We will look at the Lock Screen changes next.

Customised Lock Screens

Multiple Custom Lock Screens (iPhone Only)

iOS 16 has brought several changes to Lock Screens for the iPhone. (Not available on the iPad at this point.)

The first of these is the ability to create multiple custom Lock Screens and be able to easily switch between them.

The custom Lock Screens can have different designs. Each can have a different background colour, graphics, a single photo or a series of photos, customized font and more.

Lock Screens can be customized and added by touching and holding on the current Lock Screen.

Choosing the + symbol at bottom right provides the third image below – to choose the style/look/photo/etc for the new Lock Screen. Or swipe right to left through

your existing Lock Screens until you find the **Add New** screen, with a 🔵 in the middle. Tap the + to choose one of the Wallpaper options provided.

In the rightmost example above, I chose one of the **Suggested Photos** – the one with the kitten.

I can swipe from right to left to see different 'filters' for the selected phot and can **Pinch to Crop** – to zoom the photo in and out and position the subject.

Tapping the time shows the screen on the right, which allows me to tap to choose the time's the font and colour.

Customised Lock Screens

Add Widgets to Lock Screens

Each Lock screen can now also have a set of Widgets showing, providing snippets of information from certain apps. Tap ADD WIDGETS

This will give the options shown in the second screen above - giving the range of Widgets that are available. Only certain apps/features provide such widgets.

Scroll down to see the list of apps that can provide widgets. Tap to see the Widgets they offer – some bigger than the others. Tap to choose.

At most, you can have 4 small widgets – less if you choose any of the larger sizes.

Pair Home Screen Wallpaper with a Lock Screen

Once you have added finished customizing your screen, tap the **Add** option at top right

You will then be given the option to choose you're the Home Screen wallpaper that is paired with your Lock Screen.

Choose **Set as Wallpaper Pair** to have a blurred version of the lock screen image as the Home Screen background. Or choose to **Customise Home Screen** (which we won't cover here).

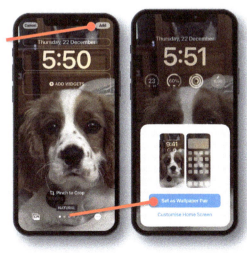

Customised Lock Screens

Link the Lock Screen to a Focus type

Once you have set up your Lock Screen, you can then choose to link that Lock Screen to a Focus type (if desired – not mandatory)

Tap **Focus** at the bottom of your Lock Screen (while it is still in 'Edit' mode) and choose which Focus should be linked.

Note that the Lock Screen associated with a Focus type can also be chose from **Settings -> Focus**. See earlier in this book for the description of these settings.

Complete customisation

Choose **Customise** to make any other changes to your Lock Screen.

If you have completed customisations, simply tap the screen to take it out of the Edit mode.

Switch between your Lock Screens

To change Lock Screens manually, touch and hold the Lock Screen (to get it back into Edit mode, then swipe right to left (or left to right) to move between your screens.

Tap the screen again to select the currently visible Lock Screen and exit 'edit' mode.

Get to know Siri

If you are not using Siri on your iPhone or iPad, you may be missing lots of useful features and ways that your device can help you in your day-to-day life.

What is Siri

Siri is your personal assistant, provided by your Apple device.

Whenever you are connected to the Internet, you can use Siri to perform lots of tasks on your iPad or iPhone – tasks that would otherwise usually require multiple taps and perhaps lots of typing. Instead, you talk to Siri.

How to Activate Siri

How Siri is activated depends on the model of iPad or iPhone you have.

- **If you <u>do</u> have a Home Button** - hold the Home Button for about a second

- **If you <u>don't</u> have a Home Button** - hold the sleep/wake switch for about second (see above for position of this switch)

- **If you have enabled a particular Setting (covered shortly):** Say 'Hey Siri'

The indication that Siri has been activated is the appearance of a circle at the bottom of your device, as indicated above.

Get to know Siri

Siri doesn't seem to work on my device

For Siri to work on your device, it must first be enabled. To check the Siri settings, go to **Settings -> Siri & Search**.

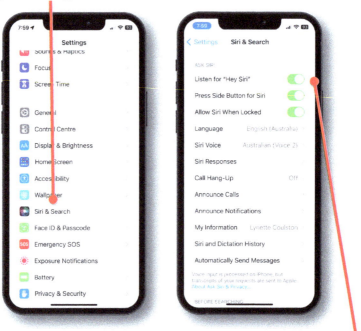

If you want to be able to use Siri 'hands-free', turn on the **Listen for "Hey Siri"** setting (more on this soon).

Also ensure that the follow option is enabled (depending on your device type)

- **Press Side Button for Siri** - if you <u>don't</u> have a Home Button OR

- **Press Home for Siri** - if you <u>do</u> have a Home Button.

You will see you also have the option to **Allow Siri When Locked**. If you need to be especially cautious about security, turn this setting to off (not green).

Although, you may wish to leave this turned on if you want to take full advantage of Hey Siri at times when you can't touch your phone (times when it will probably be locked) - for example, driving, cooking, etc.

In these Settings for Siri, you will also see that you can change Siri's **Language**, and even change Siri's voice and accent (in **Siri Voice**).

Get to know Siri

Siri doesn't let me finish!

If you find that Siri is not giving you enough of a chance to say your piece (i.e. if a pause in your speech causes Siri to stop listening too soon), just continue holding down the Home Button or Sleep Switch (whichever is applicable) until you have finished speaking.

When you let go, Siri will do 'his/her' thing.

'Hey Siri' for hands-free use of your assistant

If you have newer iPhone or iPad Pro, you can set your device up so that you can activate Siri by saying the words **"Hey Siri"**.

This can be very handy when you are in a situation where you can't touch your phone – for example, when driving.

But beware that Siri may hear 'Hey Siri' from people other than you or may mis-hear words that sound like that phrase! It sometimes even activates (from my Watch) when a tap is running!

Make sure Siri knows who you are

Some commands require that Siri knows who you are and where you live. For example, if you ask Siri to 'Give me directions home', Siri needs to know where Home is.

Make sure you have an entry in your **Contacts** for yourself, and that this Contact card includes your address.

In Siri & Search settings, tap **My Information** and select your own Contact card.

Let's look at some handy Siri commands and questions

Contact people
- Call my husband
- Call my mum
- Facetime Sharon
- Call my husband
- Dial 1300 885 420
- Email John Smith subject Today's Class
- Tell my husband I am running 10 minutes late.

Useful questions
- What song is playing
- Is it going to rain soon?
- What is the current temperature?
- What's the forecast for tomorrow?
- What's on at the movies?
- What is the tallest building in the world?
- How tall is the Eiffel Tower?

Math and conversions

- Calculate 254 plus 697?
- What is 25 by 50?
- What is the exchange rate for Australian to US dollars?
- How much is $259 Australian in US dollars?
- Convert 375 Fahrenheit to Celsius
- Convert 35 miles to kilometres
- Convert 165cm into inches

Search the web

- Search for chicken recipes with mushroom and capsicums
- Search Google for images of spring flowers
- Search Google for the nearest Caltex service station
- Search the web for information about Windows Cortana

Ask about Distance, Directions and Traffic

- What is the distance between here and Sydney?
- How far is it to my mum's?
- Give me directions to Sharon's
- Give me directions to Chadstone Shopping Centre
- Give me directions to work
- Give me directions to Margaret Jones *(assuming Margaret and her address are in your Contacts)*
- Where can I get petrol?
- Where can a get pizza? (Also ask "How far away it is?")

Staying organised

- Remind me tomorrow at 8am to pay the electricity bill.
- Remind me on Friday October 13th to look out for black cats
- Remind me when I get to Cameron Close to speak to Ray
- Remind me at 8am every morning to take my tablet
- Set up a doctor's appointment for 3pm on Wednesday
- Schedule Pilates every Wednesday morning at 9am
- Schedule Book Group on the first Tuesday of every month at 7pm

Dates, Times, timers and alarms

- What time is it?
- What time is it in London?
- What's the date today?
- What's the date on Saturday?
- What date is Easter next year
- What day is Christmas next year
- Set a timer for 30 minutes
- Stop the timer
- Resume the timer
- Set an alarm for 6:30am every weekday
- Wake me at 8am on weekends
- Wake me in 30 minutes
- Show my alarms
- Turn off my 8am alarm
- Turn off all alarms

Clever Siri!

- Show me the photos I took in London this year
- Show me the photos from last Christmas
- Remind about this when I get home (perhaps a draft email that you hadn't sent)
- Remind me about this when I get to my car
- What's the weather like today in London?

Get to know Siri

Helping Siri to understand you

You can help Siri to better understand you by offering corrections whenever it gets things wrong!

If there is a name that Siri doesn't seem to understand, you can add a 'phonetic' version of that name in the Contact card for the person. (We cover the Contacts app in a separate iTandCoffee guide.)

Another way to improve and correct Siri is to look at the translation that appears when you have finished speaking.

Once you stop speaking, Siri will show the text of what you sent at the top of the screen. If it is correct, just tap the action that appears on the right of the text – which in the above case is **Send.**

But if there is any error or need for changes, tap in that box of text and make the necessary edits before choosing the action shown.

Some Typing and Editing Tips

There is a separate iTandCoffee guide on the whole topic of typing and editing, but it is worth covering a few key tips as part of this Guided Tour. In the below descriptions, we refer to the 'cursor'. The cursor is the vertical line that shows your current typing position.

Avoid typing whenever possible!

It is not only Siri that can save you from lots of typing on your iPad and iPhone.

Any iPad or iPhone that has Siri also has a 'dictation' feature that is available whenever you see the keyboard.

Look for the 'Microphone' key on the left-hand side of the Space bar on iPads and iPhones with a Home Button (see image below left), or at bottom right of iPhones without a Home Button (see image below right).

This key allows you to dictate your text instead of typing. It can be an amazing time saver, and worth learning how to use.

Dictation changes

New in iOS/iPadOS 16: While you are dictating, the keyboard will now remain on the screen, so that you can type any words that you know might be hard for the dictation tool to interpret.

While you are in dictation mode, the microphone will have a dark grey background.

Just speak slowly and clearly, and it is best to 'speak' any punctuation that is required. Use the words 'new line' to request the inserting of a line feed, 'full stop' to add a full stop.

In saying that, in iOS/iPadOS 16, the dictation tool has improved and will attempt to insert punctuation itself if you don't do this. And it does a pretty good job.

When you are finished dictating, the microphone again – so that it is no longer a dark grey.

Some Typing and Editing Tips

Tips for editing text

No matter what, you are not going to avoid using your iPad and iPhone's on-screen keyboard to type your messages, Notes, documents, and search phrases.

If you have typed a very long sentence or paragraph – and find you have an error in the middle of what you typed – the last thing you want to do is backspace to the point where the error occurred, and then have to retype.

Here are a few editing tips that might help:

Select a word

Double-tap a word to select that word.

Select a whole paragraph

Triple-tap on any word in a paragraph to select the whole paragraph. This is three quick taps on the same paragraph

What can you do with selected text?

You can then just type something to replace the selected word or paragraph.

Or press the ⌫ or **delete** key to delete the word paragraph

You can also touch and drag the 'dots' that surround the selected word or paragraph to expand the selected area.

The top left dot can be dragged to the left and upwards, and the bottom right dot can be dragged to the right and downwards.

Below is an example of such an expansion of the selected area.

You will also notice a black bar above any selected text, which provides various options that can be applied to the selection – Cut, Copy, Paste, **B***I*U (bold / italics / underline options) and much more.

Some Typing and Editing Tips

Move to a point in your text (i.e. set your 'cursor position')

As described at the start of this chapter, the **cursor** is the vertical line that shows the current typing position. Here are some ways that you can set that cursor position.

Touch and hold on the space set your cursor position.

The first is to **touch and hold on the space bar** on the keyboard until the keys disappear.

Without lifting, move your finger around the keyboard area and you will see the cursor move accordingly.

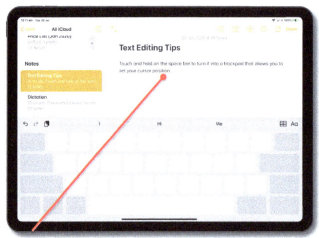

Let go when the cursor is in the required position.

In the example above, if I start typing, the letters will appear after the 'o' in 'position'.

Alternatively, in iOS/iPadOS 16, Apple has re-introduced the ability to just touch and move your finger over text - and see a bubble above to show the word on which you are positioned.

In the example on the right, my finger was on top of the word 'previous', so there is a bubble above showing this positioning, and that the cursor is after the 'v'.

As I move my finger, the content of this bubble changes, allowing me to see exactly where the cursor is positioned. I let go when I am at the required cursor position.

Some Typing and Editing Tips

Discover 'Undo' on the iPad

The Numeric keyboard – which appears when you tap the   key - has the  **Undo** key. This is very handy for when you need to undo one or more things you have just typed, moved, deleted, etc.

The 'undo' symbol also appears in the iPad's 'predictive text bar that – which is the bar above the keyboard.

Tap ↶ to undo, and to 're-do' something that was ↷ 'undone'.

Shake to Undo – for both iPhone and iPad

There is no such key or symbol for Undo on the iPhone keyboard.

Instead, there are a couple of gestures/actions you can use to Undo your most recent action/typing – gestures that apply on both the iPhone and iPad.

Shake the iPhone (or iPad)! Yes, just give it a shake. A confirmation message will appear – tap Undo when you see that message to confirm.

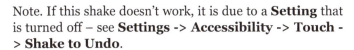

Note. If this shake doesn't work, it is due to a **Setting** that is turned off – see **Settings -> Accessibility -> Touch -> Shake to Undo**.

To **'re-do'** what you just 'undid', shake the phone again and choose the **Re-do** option.

Three-finger Swipe to Undo

Swipe left with three fingers. This will not give you any confirmation screen – it will Undo straight away.

To **'re-do'** what you just 'undid', swipe the other way (left to right) with 3 fingers.

Three-finger tap to Undo

NEW in iOS/iPadOS 16: There is now an additional Undo/Redo gesture.

Tap the screen with three fingers at once, to see a bar appear at the top of the screen.
This gives you the Undo ↶ and Redo ↷ symbols.

Sharing and Printing

The Share symbol and menu

There is a very special symbol available in many apps on the iPad and iPhone, one that allows you to choose to 'share' or do something else with content on your device.

It is the Share symbol, which provides the Share menu.

The content of the Share menu will differ per App, but here is a sample from the Photos app.

The key functions available in the Share menu for the content that you have selected are:

- Airdrop the content to another nearby Apple device
- Send the content in an email
- Send the item/s in a Message
- Add the content to a Note
- Copy the content (so that you can 'paste' elsewhere)
- Print
- Open in another app
- And much more, depending on the App.

Print from the Share menu

You may not be aware that your iPad and iPhone both have the capability to print.

As long as you have a **Wi-Fi enabled** printer that is connected to the same Wi-Fi network as your iPad/iPhone, then you can print all sorts of things – photos, web pages, emails, Notes, documents and more.

The **Print** option can be found in the **Share** menu.

Scroll down through the options in the list to find Print. Tap this option to see the Printer Options screen (see image above right).

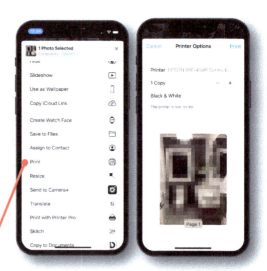

Sharing and Printing

If no printer is shown in the **Printer** field, tap that field and tap the name of the your printer (which should appear, but only if you are connected to the same Wi-Fi network as the printer).

Then tap Print at top right to print your document.

Or, before you print, you can adjust the number of copies and other features of your printout before printing. The options that appear are dependent on the features of your printer.

Print from Mail

Full details about using the Mail app are available in a separate iTandCoffee guide. For now, we will just look at how you can Print a mail message.

While most apps provide the Share symbol and menu, this symbol is not available in the Mail app.

Instead, the **Print** option is found in the menu that appears when you tap the **Reply** symbol

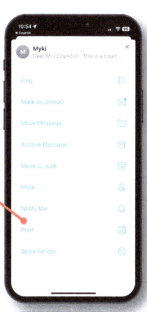

The Reply symbol is found

- at bottom right of a message on the iPad OR

- in the bottom menu bar when viewing the message on the iPhone

Drag up to scroll down through the options, to find the **Print** option.

Other places to find the Share & Print options

If you don't see the Share symbol, another symbol to look for is some dots – perhaps with a circle around them.

Here is such a symbol in the Pages app.

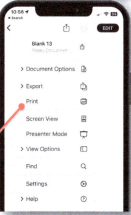

In that app, the Print option is found by tapping that symbol.

Take a Photo of your Screen!

Taking a photo of your device's screen can be so handy when you don't have access to a printer but need to keep a record of something that is on your iPad or iPhone screen.

If you have an iPhone or iPad <u>with</u> a Home Button.

- Press the **Sleep/Wake Switch** and the **Home** button at the same time (just a quick press).

For iPhones and iPads <u>without</u> a Home Button

- Press the Sleep Switch and the Volume Up buttons at the same time.

Take a Photo of your Screen!

A small 'thumbnail' of your screenshot will then appear at the bottom left of the screen. This thumbnail will disappear after a few seconds if you do nothing, and the photo of the screen will be saved to your Photos library.

(We cover the Photos app in a separate iTandCoffee guide.)

Here's what you can do with that thumbnail while it is still on the screen.

- Swipe left on the thumbnail to get it off the screen (and save it to your Photos library).

- Touch and hold briefly, then let go of the thumbnail, to see the Share menu and share the screenshot (or use one of the other options provided by the Share screen).

- Tap it to add drawings or text, crop the image and more (a feature called Markup). This is so handy when you need to send a photo to someone and highlight something about that photo. The bar of 'drawing tools' appears along the bottom. Tap any then use your finger (or Apple Pencil if you have one for your iPad) to apply your 'markup'.

- When finished 'marking up' or just viewing your photo of the screen, you can

  o Choose the Share symbol to share the photo of the screen (known as a 'screenshot') – or access any of the other options from the Share menu, such as Print or Copy.

  o Choose **Done** and choose *Save to Photos* if you want to keep the photo in your Photos library, *Save to Files* to save to iCloud Drive or your device's 'local' storage or choose one of the Delete options shown (or choose to delete it using the 'trash can' symbol towards top right.)

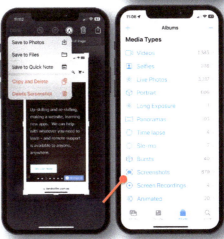

To easily find the screenshot you just took, along with ones you've taken and saved before, go to **Photos -> Albums** and tap the **Screenshots** album, which can be found by scrolling down to the section headed **Media Types**.

Managing Your Device's Storage

Our iPads and iPhones have a limit to how much they can store.

Unfortunately, it is not possible to expand this storage capacity – we are stuck with the amount that we purchased.

For older devices with the minimum capacity of 16GB (or even 32GB), managing storage can quite be a challenge.

How do you find out how much data your device is using, and just where this all data is being used?

iPhone Storage / iPad Storage

The **iPhone Storage** (or **iPad Storage**) option of **Settings -> General** is the place to go to work out what is taking up space on your device.

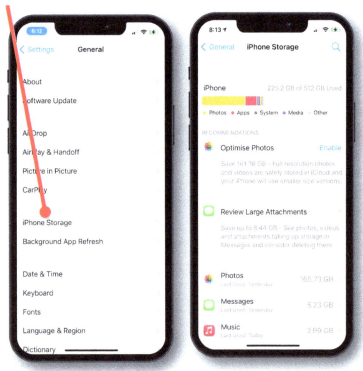

The top area of iPhone/iPad Storage screen shows how much storage has been used and how much is still available. The bar along the top shows the various types of data that are using up your space.

Managing Your Device's Storage

Recommendations for freeing up storage

You may then see some **Recommendations** for freeing up storage on your device. The recommendations you see here depend on some other settings on your device.

Below that you will see the list of the apps that are on your iPad or iPhone. The biggest users of data are shown at the top of the list.

The most common Recommendations are to **Optimise Photos**, **Review Large Attachments**, and **Offload Apps**.

The **Optimise Photos** option relates to iCloud Photos and utilising a feature that removes the full versions of photos from your device and only stores cutdown versions. (Refer to iTandCoffee book **The Comprehensive Guide to iCloud** for more details about iCloud and whether you should choose Enable if this option appears.)

The Messages recommendation will appear if you have some large photos and/or videos in Messages you have sent or received. If you were the one who sent these photos/videos, they are probably copies of what you have stored in your Photos – so can, most likely, be safely deleted from Messages to save space.

When I tap the option to **Review Large Attachments** on my own iPhone 12, there are quite a lot of large videos that I can delete – as shown in the screen shot on the right.

Deletion of items in this list is achieved by swiping the item from right to left and tapping **Delete**.

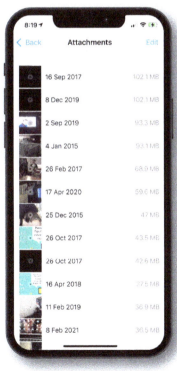

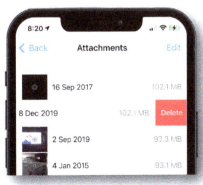

121

Managing Your Device's Storage

Storage used by individual apps

Below any Recommendations is a list of the apps on your device, ordered according to the storage space that they use.

The total size of each app (including the data that it stores) is shown on the right side of the list of apps. Also included is an indication of when the app was last used.

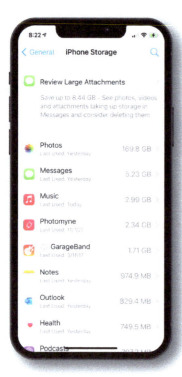 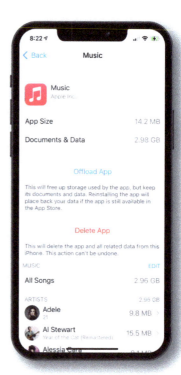

For each of the apps shown in the list, touch on the App name to view more details about the App and its data usage.

For example, the total amount of storage used my Music app on my iPhone is 2.99 GB.

Tapping on that App I can see that the App itself is only 14.2MB – but the data it stores is 2.98GB.

If I decided that I did not need to use this App any more, I can delete it completely – along with all its data – by choosing Delete App.

Managing Your Device's Storage

Deleting stored content

If I tap on the Podcasts app, I can see any downloaded Podcasts that are stored on my device and how much space they use.

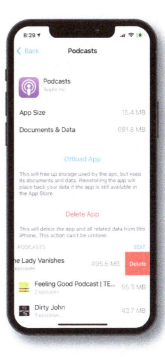

Swiping right to left across the Podcast title provides the **Delete** option – tap this to remove the Podcast, which will still be available to be 'streamed' from the Podcasts apps.

The same applies for other apps like Music, and TV – simply swipe right to left on any stored content to remove that item and free up storage.

Offloading Apps

In some cases, you temporarily need to 'offload' an app to free up some storage space – but don't want to lose the data you have stored on your device for that app. So you don't want to **Delete** the app, as that would delete its data.

In this case, you can instead choose to **Offload App**.

This removes the App, but leaves its data behind – so that, when you re-download the app from the App Store, all your data is still there, ready and waiting.

In the example below, the iMovie app has been 'offloaded' – so shows a cloud symbol.

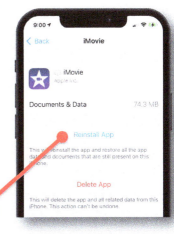

To get it back, I tap on the app in the list and choose the **Reinstall App** option

Securing your device - Passcode Lock

Why set a passcode?

It is essential to **set a Passcode Lock** on your iPad and iPhone, to keep anyone who takes your i-Device without permission from accessing your information.

It's just like having a deadlock on your front door!

Without a Passcode Lock, your iPad or iPhone may be used to gain access to all sorts of financial and personal information about you – accounts, passwords, and more could be stolen or maliciously used.

Your mail account could be used to perform 'password resets' of your online accounts, thereby locking you out of these accounts and allowing all sorts of damage to be done.

Depending on the Settings on your device, you may be unwittingly saving away the login credentials to various websites and online services. Without a Passcode, any person could access your online accounts.

If your device has a Passcode, when you want to unlock your iPad, you will be asked to provide your Passcode - unless you have also recorded a fingerprint (Touch ID) or your face Face ID (we'll cover this shortly).

We will also cover shortly how to avoid having to enter this Passcode EVERY time you want to use your device, if you choose not to record a fingerprint or Face ID.

Even if your device has a fingerprint sensor (or Face ID), it is still necessary to set up a Passcode. The Passcode is required every time you power up your device – and for certain other activities. So it is essential that you don't forget it!

Your passcode can be one of three types:

* A Standard Passcode of 6 numbers
* A Numeric passcode of 4 numbers or more
* A Complex Passcode – can any combination of letters, numbers and symbols.

Complex passcodes are much, much more secure than simple 4-digit passcodes. The more letters and numbers, the better the security.

In fact, an easily guessed 4-digit or 6-digit password is as bad as no password – so make sure you choose something that can't be easily guessed.

Securing your device - Passcode Lock

To set up your Passcode

Go to

- **Settings -> Face ID & Passcode** if your device supports Face ID.

- **Settings ->Touch ID & Passcode** if your device supports Touch ID.

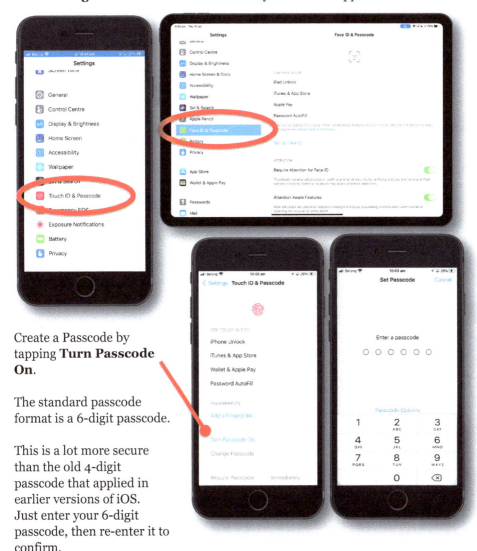

Create a Passcode by tapping **Turn Passcode On**.

The standard passcode format is a 6-digit passcode.

This is a lot more secure than the old 4-digit passcode that applied in earlier versions of iOS. Just enter your 6-digit passcode, then re-enter it to confirm.

Securing your device - Passcode Lock

"I don't want a 6-digit passcode!"

To set up a different style of Passcode, tap Passcode Options, which can be found just above the on-screen numeric keypad.

Choose the style of Passcode you would like to create then enter that passcode twice.

A 'Custom Numeric Code' can be any number of digits. A 'Custom Alphanumeric Code' can be a combination of letters and number, of any length.

The more digits/characters, the more secure your Passcode will be.

It is highly recommended that you do not choose to use a 4-Digit Numeric Code only.

If you have set up something called Two Factor Authentication for your Apple account, you will then be asked to confirm your Apple ID's password (assuming you have signed in with an Apple ID when you set up your device).

(Note. We don't cover the topic of Apple IDs in this guide. Refer to the guide **The Comprehensive Guide to iCloud** for more information about Apple ID's and iCloud.)

Choose the 'require passcode' interval

Ideally, you will set your device up to use Touch ID or Face ID (whichever is available)

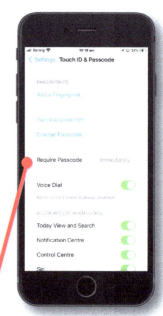

If you choose not to utilise these features, it can be frustrating having to enter the Passcode every time the device locks.

For devices on which there are no fingerprints or Face ID recorded, it is possible to set a 'delay' so that your passcode is only required once the device has been asleep for a period that you specify.

Touch on **Require Passcode** and choose a 'delay' interval.

Securing your device - Passcode Lock

Shorter delays are more secure. For example, setting a delay of 1 minute means that once your device has been asleep for a minute, you will be required to enter a passcode to unlock it.

Within that minute however, you (or anyone else in possession of your device) can unlock it without entering a passcode.

On the iPad, the available **Require Password** intervals are much longer than the iPhone, probably in recognition that the iPhone is more likely to end up in the wrong hands than the iPad.

Add your fingerprint/s

If your device has a Home Button with fingerprint sensor or if you are the owner of a newer model iPad Air (which has the fingerprint sensor on the sleep/wake switch), then you can also save one or more of your fingerprints so that, in future, you can unlock the device using any of those fingerprints.

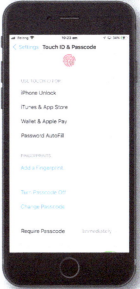

Select **Add a Fingerprint ...**, then follow the instructions to 'record' your fingerprint. Repeat this for each finger that you wish to use (tapping **Add a Fingerprint** ... for each finger you wish to 'record').

Securing your device - Passcode Lock

Tap on each fingerprint to change the name of that fingerprint – so that you can identify the different prints if ever you need. Just remove the default name by tapping the x then type the new name for that fingerprint (eg. Right Index).

You can see in the rightmost image above that you also have the **Delete Fingerprint** option – to remove any fingerprint that is not working properly or has perhaps been added by one of your kids!

Set up Face ID

Tap **Set up Face ID**, then follow the on-screen instructions – which involve positioning your face in the frame provided, and slowly moving your head in a circle while looking at yourself in the frame.

Securing your device - Passcode Lock

Select what your Touch ID or Face ID can be used for

Once you have set up Touch ID or Face ID, go to **USE TOUCH ID FOR** (or **USE FACE ID FOR**) at the top of the Passcode options.

Choose what 'approvals' you would like to control using your Touch ID or Face ID.

If you have set up this quick/easy method of authentication, it is worth enabling each of the options shown here.

If there are any apps that can use Touch ID or Face ID (for example your banking apps or authenticator apps), these will be listed under the **Other Apps** option.

Do I have to have a Passcode if I set up Touch ID or Face ID?

A Passcode must still be set for your device, even if you use these other forms of authentication. It is the Passcode that will encrypt all the data on your device and prevent anyone from accessing your data without that passcode.

Your Passcode will be requested every time your turn your device back on, after a 'force restart', if you invoke the Emergency SOS screen, if there are multiple failed attempts to unlock using Face ID or Touch ID, and in various other places.

A BIG WARNING! Do Not Forget Your Passcode!

There is no way of retrieving your device's Passcode if you lose it, and your iPad or iPhone will have to be restored to factory settings. This will result in the loss of all data that you have not backed up or sync'd with iCloud (or another cloud service), potentially including precious photos.

Once you have set a passcode, if you go back to **Settings-> Touch ID & Passcode/Face ID & Passcode**, you will be asked to first enter the Passcode to open those settings.

Securing your device - Passcode Lock

A Password Safe that is protected by your Passcode

As already mentioned, it is **<u>HIGHLY RECOMMENDED</u>** that you set a Passcode Lock on your device.

However, if

- you choose to NOT set a Passcode Lock on your device, you remove it,
- if others know your Passcode Lock, or
- someone else has stored their fingerprint / Face ID on your device,

make sure that your device is **not saving your online account login details** (including passwords).

Go to **Settings -> Passwords** to see what is saved there.

If you DO have a passcode set, you will be asked to enter it to access your Passwords list

Alternatively use your Face ID or Touch ID (whichever applies).

You will then see your list of 'Saved' passwords that Safari can use to 'autofill' on certain web pages and in certain apps.

Tap any item in the list to view the username and password for that item.

If you have details in this list that you wish to remove, you can delete some or all of them.

Securing your device - Passcode Lock

Delete 'remembered' passwords

To delete individual items in the list of Passwords, swipe from right to left on the item to reveal the **Delete** option. Tap this to delete the remembered details.

Alternatively, choose Edit at top right, and then touch the circle on the left of each item in the list that you want to delete to 'tick' these items.

Then choose Delete at top left to remove the selected items from the list.

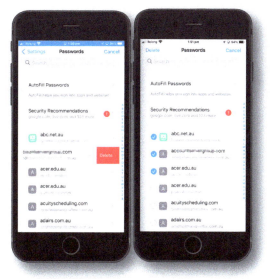

Add other passwords

You can use this area of Settings as your 'Password Safe', for recording passwords that are then protected by your device Passcode/Face ID/Touch ID.

To add a password, tap the + at top right

Then fill in the details of the website, username and password and choose **Done** at top right.

Your Device's Battery

Understanding Battery Usage

A key issue we all face is ensuring that our device has sufficient charge when we need it – so managing the battery usage is very important.

The iPad and iPhone Settings provide an option called Battery, that allows you to see what has been using up your battery, offers suggestions for improving your battery life, and (for the iPhone) provides a **Battery Health** option for checking if your device's battery needs attention.

Show Battery Percentage on newer iPhones

New in iOS 16 for iPhones without a Home Button is that you can now choose to show the **Battery Percentage** (first option in image above left) on top of the battery symbol at top right. Previously, you only got the graphic without the %.

See what Apps are using all your power

Scroll down to see a graphic of your battery usage, and to view the apps that are using the most battery. Tap on any of the bars in the chart to see the apps that were in use at that time.

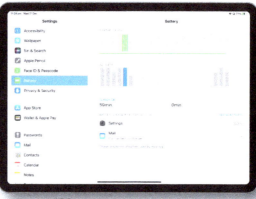

Saving your Battery Life

Check if your battery needs replacing

The **Battery Health & Charging** option on the iPhone helps to give insight into whether your iPhone's battery may have deteriorated to a point where it needs replacing.

As an example, the iPhone shown in the screen on the right has a maximum capacity of 81% - so the battery is not now capable of holding a full day's charge and will need replacing soon.

As shown in the image on the right, if your battery is seriously degraded, you will see a message here indicating that a service (i.e. replacement) is needed.

When you are low on power

Sometimes, you need to ensure your battery doesn't die on you!

One of the key ways of reducing your power usage is to dim your screen's brightness – from **Settings -> Display & Brightness** or using the brightness control in the **Control Centre**.

Also make sure that your device auto-locks (as described earlier) after as short a period as possible – again, to stop the screen's display from wasting battery.

Fortunately, the **Low Power Mode** feature will alert you if your battery level drops to 20% and provides the option to switch off or reduce some functions to preserve the battery.

As described on the Settings screen, **Low Power Mode** "temporarily reduces background activity, like downloads and mail fetch until you can fully charge your iPhone/iPad".

Just press Continue when you see the message advising about low battery level, to turn on this battery conservation mode.

For other times when you need to preserve the battery usage, you can manually turn on **Low Power Mode** from **Settings -> Battery**.

The Control Centre can also include a control for Low Power Mode 🔋, making it easier to quickly turn this mode on and off.

Visit **Settings -> Control Centre** to add this control if it does not already appear in your Control Centre.

About your Device

What is the name of your iPad or iPhone?

Is it identifiable from another iPhone or iPad when you need to use features like Airdrop or Personal Hotspot.

What is stored on your device? What Model is it, where do you find its Serial Number, and what is its storage capacity?

These questions can all be answered – and your device's name changed – in an area of **Settings** called **About**.

Just go to **Settings -> General -> About**.

About gives a general overview of the content on your iPad/iPhone – how many Songs, Videos, Photos, Applications you have on the device, the capacity of your device and how much of that is currently available, what Version of iOS/iPadOS you are currently running, Model Number, Serial Number, and various other more technical information.

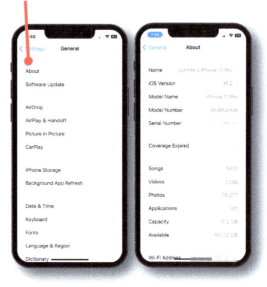

Change device's name

Importantly, this is where you can **change the name of your device**.

Touch > next to **Name** (top option), then remove the existing name and replace it with the name you prefer for your device.

Save away your device's information

Given that the **About** settings page shows you lots of important information about the identity of your device (for example, its Serial Number), it is a good idea to take a screen shot of this screen and perhaps print and keep it somewhere for safe keeping.

Then, if your device is lost, stolen or broken, the information you have saved away may help identify the device.

Versions & Upgrades/Updates

What are iOS and iPadOS

As described earlier on, the software or 'operating' system that runs everything on your iPhone and iPod touch is known as iOS. On iPads, it is now called iPadOS. (Note. Some older iPads still run iOS and cannot be upgraded to iPadOS.)

iOS/iPadOS Updates and Upgrades

Apple **upgrades** iOS/iPadOS on an annual basis, to add new features and improve existing features. For example, the lastest upgrade was from iOS/iPadOS 15 to iOS/iPadOS 16.

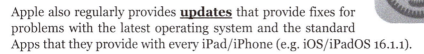

Apple also regularly provides **updates** that provide fixes for problems with the latest operating system and the standard Apps that they provide with every iPad/iPhone (e.g. iOS/iPadOS 16.1.1).

It is important to know that some earlier models of the iPad and iPhone cannot be updated beyond a certain iOS version.

How do you know there is an update/upgrade?

The easiest rule of thumb is that if you receive a notification on your **Settings** icon then your device is eligible to update or upgrade to the newest version.

When such an update release is available, you may see a ⓵ on the **Settings** icon on the Home Screen.

Or you may read about it in the iTandCoffee Newsletter – subscribe at www.itandcoffee.com.au/newsletter.

At any time, you can got to **Settings -> General -> Software Update**, to see if any such update (or upgrade) is available.

Should you update/upgrade?

Different rules apply for **updates** vs **upgrades**.

It is always a good idea to keep your device as up to date as possible. When you receive notification of an **update**, it is worth downloading and installing this update as soon as possible – unless there is negative press about it that indicates something is wrong with the update. Wait a couple of days at least to be sure. You can always Google something like "any problems with iOS 16.2?" and see what articles have been published about the update before proceeding.

For **upgrades**, it is definitely worth waiting a few weeks to let the 'dust settle' on the upgrade and allow other people to discover the problems. There will always be inevitable 'fix' releases shortly after an **upgrade**.

iOS Versions & Upgrades/Updates

Of course, if you are really keen, you can 'jump in' early and install the **upgrade** – especially if you are desperate for any of the new features that are advertised as included in that upgrade.

How do I upgrade or update when I see the '1'

If your **Settings** app is showing a ● on it, it's quite simple really - just follow the 1's! (Although that may indicate that there is something else that needs to be set up or confirmed, so cannot always be relied on to show updates/upgrades. Do pay attention to it regardless of what it is indicating – as it shows that something needs to be done.)

However, this ● doesn't necessarily appear as soon as there is an update available – so if you have heard of an update/upgrade, then you can check if it is available to you using the steps below.

Touch on the **Settings** app. If there was a ● on the app on the Home Screen, you will see that the **General** option also has a ● next to it.

Tap **General**, then the second option in the list, **Software Update** (which might also have a ● on it).

If there is an available update or upgrade, you will see a **Download and Install** option (or it may just say **Install** if the update/upgrade file has already been downloaded to your device). Above right is an example of such a screen, for an earlier update of iOS.

Tap this to initiate the software download/ installation. You may need to enter your device's passcode and agree to terms and conditions.

You might also notice that there is an **ALSO AVAILABLE** heading at the bottom of the screen – reflecting the availability of an **Upgrade**. If you are ready to apply this Upgrade, tap this option to proceed. There is no need to apply the Update (if one is showing) before you do these. The Upgrade will include any of the fixes or new features from the update.

iOS Versions & Upgrades/Updates

Depending on the size of the update/upgrade, and on the speed of your internet, this process may take quite a while! Your device will restart itself as part of this process and show a progress bar for the update.

When the device is available again, you will need to enter your Passcode to unlock the device and continue using it.

But before you update …

Make sure your device is connected to power, and that you are on a Wi-Fi network.

It is also **strongly recommended** that your device has been **Backed Up** before you update or upgrade it.

(Details of how to ensure that your device is backed up automatically to your iCloud are covered in a separate guide – **The Comprehensive Guide to iCloud**.)

You will also need to have sufficient storage on your iPad or iPhone to perform the upgrade. If you don't, you will need to clear some space first.

Refer earlier in this guide for information about how to check your storage usage and how to delete or offload Apps and data that you don't need.

Can my device run iOS/iPadOS 16

If you have an older device, you may not be able to upgrade to the latest version of the operating system.

For iOS/iPadOS 16, your iPhone must be an iPhone 8/iPhone X (released 2017) or newer. This means iPhone 6S and 7 series, and the original iPhone SE (and older devices) are no longer able to be upgraded.

All iPads that are without a Home Button can be upgraded to iPadOS 16.

For those iPads <u>with</u> a Home button, your iPad must be at least a 5th Generation iPad (released 2017), an iPad Air Gen 3 (2019) or newer, or an iPad Pro (any model).

Troubleshooting

If an app is misbehaving...

The first thing to try when an app is not behaving itself is to close it from the multi-taskings screen.

Bring up this screen, using the method described earlier.

Then, **swipe the app upwards** to close it.

This will normally resolve whatever ailed the misbehaving app.

If this doesn't help, try the next option.

What to do when your device REALLY misbehaves

If you can't get your device to respond, a major function such as mobile phone service, Wi-Fi or mobile data is not working, or some other major problem has occurred, you may need to do what is called a '**Forced Re-boot**' of your device.

This does a bit of a 'flush out' of its memory and, in most cases, helps to clear up whatever has got your device into a knot. It does not delete any of your apps or data.

Force-rebooting involves pressing two or more buttons. The applicable buttons differ for newer iPhones, as described below:

- **For iPhone 8 and 8 Plus, iPhone X Series, and later,** plus **iPhone SE second gen,** plus **iPad without Home Button**

  In quick succession: press and release the Volume Up, then press and release the Volume Down, then press and hold the Sleep switch for **about 10 seconds**. Release your hold only when the Apple appears again after the device turns off.

- **For iPad with Home Button,** plus **iPhones up to and including the iPhone 6S** plus **iPhone SE (1ˢᵗ gen):**

  Hold down the Sleep Switch **AND** the Home Button **for about 10 seconds**. Release your hold when the Apple appears again after the device turns off.

- **For iPhone 7 and 7 Plus**

  Hold down the Sleep Switch **AND** Volume Down button **for about 10 seconds.** Release your hold when the Apple appears again after the device turns off.

Troubleshooting

For all iPads and iPhones

- Wait a little while after the Apple appears, and the device will go back at the **Lock Screen**

- Unlock it as normal using your Passcode and your issue will hopefully be resolved.

- Even if you use your fingerprint or Face ID to unlock your device, you will have to enter your Passcode to re-enable this feature after re-booting (or re-starting) the device.

If an app is still misbehaving

If you find that the problem with an individual app persists even after this forced reboot, try deleting the app and re-adding it.

Standard Buttons and Symbols

Here are just some of the standard buttons you will see while using your iPad.

Button	Name	Meaning
⬆️	Share	Open a screen that provides options for sending, sharing, printing, saving – I like to call it the 'do something with' symbol.
⊙	Camera	Open a screen that displays a 'photo picker' in camera mode or allows you take a photo, scan a document or other app-specific features.
✎	Compose	Create a new email or Note
📖	Bookmarks	Show app-specific bookmarks
🔍	Search	Display a search field
+	Add	Create a new item
🗑	Trash	Delete current item
📁	Organize	Move or route an item to a destination within the app, such as a folder
↩	Reply, Forward, Print, Save	Send or route an item to another location (or save an image, document, or print)

Standard Buttons and Symbols

Button	Name	Meaning
☒	Stop	Stop current process or task or clear a field (e.g. Search field)
↻	Refresh	Force a refresh contents (use only when necessary; otherwise, it will usually refresh automatically)
▶	Play	Begin movie/video/music/media
▶▶	Fast Forward	Fast forward through movie/video/music/media
▮▮	Pause	Pause movie/video/music/media
◀◀	Rewind	Move backwards through media playback or slides
	Edit	Enter edit mode
	Cancel	Exit the editing or selection mode
	Save	Save changes and, if appropriate, exit the editing or selection mode
	Done	Exit the current mode and save changes, if any
↶	Undo	Undo the most recent action
↷	Redo	Redo the most recent undone action

Status Bar Icons

Here are the main symbols you will see in the bar at the top of your screen, along with their meaning.

Icon	Name	Meaning
✈	Aeroplane mode	Shows that Aeroplane mode is on – you can't access the Internet or use Bluetooth devices. Non-wireless features are still available.
LTE	LTE	Device is connected to the internet over a 4G LTE network
3G 4G 5G	3G / 4G/ 5G	Device is connected to the internet over a 5G, 4G or 3G network. (Note. Only iPhone 12 and newer can connect to 5G network.)
📶	WI-FI	Shows that the device has a Wi-Fi connection – the more bars, the stronger the connection. (Note that this doesn't necessarily mean you have internet – just that you are connected to a Wi-fi enabled device.)
🌙	Do Not Disturb	Device's 'Do Not Disturb' is turned on – no notification sounds will get through.
♻	Personal Hotspot	Shows that iPhone or iPad is providing a 'Personal Hotspot' to another device (which may be using the iPhone/iPad's internet data allowance).
🔄	Syncing	Shows when the iPad/iPhone is syncing with iTunes

Status Bar Icons

Icon	Name	Meaning
	Activity	Shows network or other activity. Some third-party apps use this to show an active process taking place
	Lock	Shows the iPad/iPhone is locked
	Alarm	Shows that an alarm is set
	Rotation lock	Shows that the orientation is locked (i.e. the screen won't swing around when moved).
	Location Services	Shows that an App is using Location Services (e.g. Maps)
►	Play	Shows that a song or audiobook is playing
	Bluetooth	White icon: Bluetooth is on and paired with a device, such as a keyboard. Grey icon: Bluetooth is on and paired with a device, but the device is out of range or turned off
90%	Battery	Shows the battery level and charging status.
	Airplay	Device is being mirrored onto another screen using Airplay

Other Latest Guides by iTandCoffee

- A Guided Tour of the Apple Watch

- The Comprehensive Guide to iCloud

- Keeping your Children Safe on the iPad and iPhone

- Getting to Know your Mac Series (available as individual books or as a 5-part compilation book)

    o A Guided Tour

    o Files, Folders and Finder

    o Backups, Preferences and Apps

    o All Sorts of Handy Tips and Tricks

    o The Photos App

- Boot Camp for Microsoft 365 Series

    o OneDrive

    o Excel

    o Word

www.ingramcontent.com/pod-product-compliance
Lightning Source LLC
LaVergne TN
LVHW011802070326
832902LV00025B/4605